#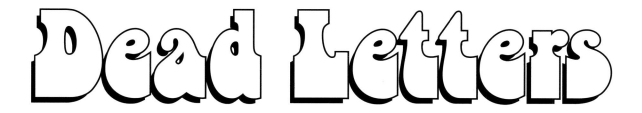

I wrote a letter I mailed in the air
Mailed it on the air indeed-e
I wrote a letter I mailed in the air
You may know by that I've got a friend somewhere.

"Viola Lee Blues," Noah Lewis, 1928;
Adapted by the Grateful Dead, recorded 1967,
performed live thirty-three times

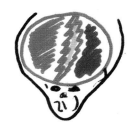

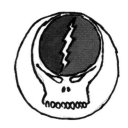

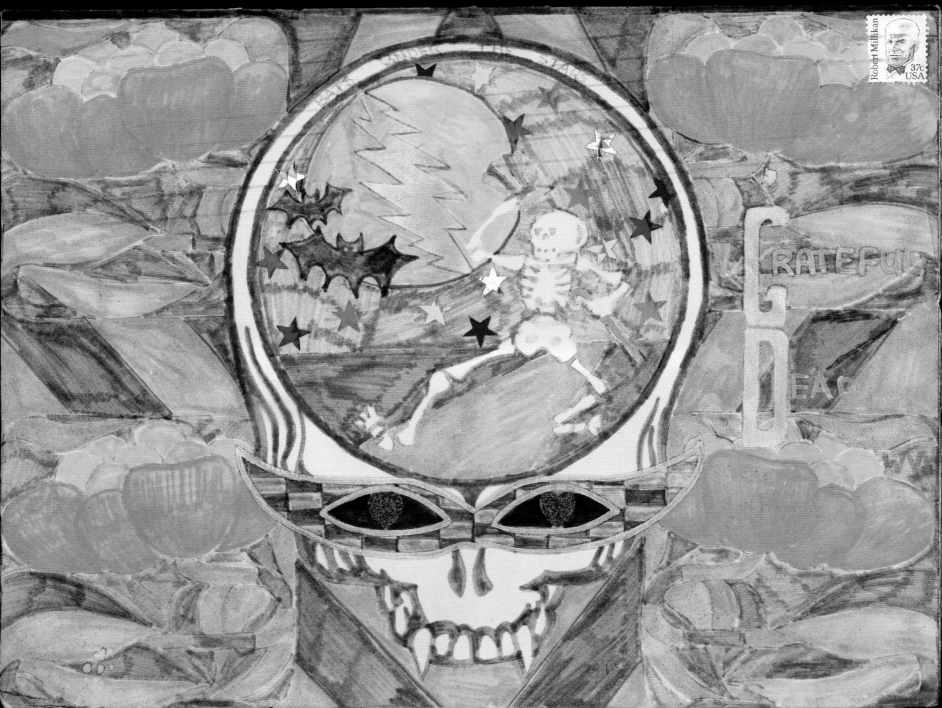

Dead Letters

The Very Best Grateful Dead Fan Mail

By Paul Grushkin

Voyageur Press

For Eileen and Calico

First published in 2011 by Voyageur Press, an imprint of MBI Publishing Company, 400 First Avenue North, Suite 300, Minneapolis, MN 55401 USA

The information in this book is true and complete to the best of our knowledge. All recommendations are made without any guarantee on the part of the author or Publisher, who also disclaims any liability incurred in connection with the use of this data or specific details.

All images from The Grateful Dead Archive, UC Santa Cruz Special Collections unless otherwise noted. All images © their respective creators. Access to all envelope art in Chapter 14 provided by GDTS TOO.

Voyageur Press recognizes that some words, model names, and designations mentioned herein are the property of the trademark holder. We use them for identification purposes only.

"Viola Lee Blues" by Noah Lewis. Used by Permission of Peer International Corporation.

Excerpts from "He's Gone," "Ripple," and "That's It for the Other One" used by permission of Ice Nine Publishing.

Voyageur Press titles are also available at discounts in bulk quantity for industrial or sales-promotional use. For details write to Special Sales Manager at MBI Publishing Company, 400 First Avenue North, Suite 300, Minneapolis, MN 55401 USA.

To find out more about our books, visit us online at www.voyageurpress.com.

Library of Congress Cataloging-in-Publication Data

Grushkin, Paul.
Dead letters : the very best Grateful Dead fan mail / Paul Grushkin.
 p. cm.
ISBN 978-0-7603-3854-4 (plc)
1. Grateful Dead (Musical group) 2. Rock musicians–United States–Correspondence. 3. Fan mail–United States. 4. Deadheads (Music fans) I. Title.
ML421.G72G78 2011
782.42166092'2–dc22

2011011666

Front cover: Mail box image *Steve Wood/Shutterstock.com*
Front and back endpapers: Mailroom image © *PoodlesRock/CORBIS*
This page: Anonymous Dead Head illustration, circa 1972. The lettering is an homage to Rick Griffin.
Back cover: Envelopes courtesy Laura Dowling

Editor: Dennis Pernu
Design Manager: LeAnn Kuhlmann
Designed by: Sandra Salamony
Layout By: Mighty Media

Printed in China

Contents

Foreword

BY BILL WALTON

It's a Miracle: Where the Band beyond Description Meets Its Match—Their Fans—and Everybody Wakes Up to Find Out That They Love Each Other

Words alone can never do justice to what is the Grateful Dead. In the all-encompassing sensations that consume us, never discount the power of the visual and sensual aspects of our dreams to convey our undying love, admiration, respect, appreciation, gratitude, and need to belong.

The world of the Grateful Dead is one of hope, joy, opportunity, celebration, pride, loyalty, curiosity, exploration, experimentation, peace, and love. These powerful and hard-driving emotions are often sadly tempered by the cold, hard realities of life. None harsher or starker than "How do I get in to the next show?"

The Grateful Dead have always inspired incredibly intense response and activation from the legions of participants in the life and times of this remarkable band of warriors from the Golden State.

Of all the countless factors that compose the Grateful Dead universe, interaction would have to be right up there at the top of the smoking crater of what makes being a part of all this so very special. Clearly we could not get what we want as fans without them. And the band certainly reached

levels that they could never get to on their own because of us.

Paul Grushkin is a Dead Head of the highest order. He's been living the dream for so long now that one might say the greatest story ever told is really his own personal biography. And now his latest masterpiece, *Dead Letters*, takes us back to another time and forgotten space. A place where we find out that everything that we dreamed, lived, and believed in really did happen—only on such a grand scale and scope that we end up asking ourselves, "Were we ever there at all?"

Dead Letters is the documentary evidence that it did and we were.

The Grateful Dead touch everything that really matters in our individual lives: art, history, music, education, information, communication, love, health, and family. Being part of this special team is truly life at its fullest and finest.

Dead Letters captures this spirit, drive, and desire perfectly with its collection of replicated documents, artifacts, and memorabilia that exquisitely chronicle not only the creative juice and

force that is the supplication of our need to be on the bus and in the game, but also the never-ending struggle of getting a ticket to ride.

When something so important in your life becomes amazingly popular with others later on down the line, it's always difficult to comprehend the magnitude of what was at all times so clear, easy, and natural for you. Things changed over time in the world of the Grateful Dead, maybe nothing as drastic for the ever-growing numbers of communicants as the difficulty in obtaining admission to the ceremonies.

From the early party days at Olompali to the free shows in the panhandle of Golden Gate Park to the ends of so many roads where finally there were so many countless thousands of people who showed up with absolutely no chance of ever getting in, the dream lived on—the dream that you were going to be able to play in the game of life that day with the Grateful Dead.

As the soaring flight began with the charge "Dead Freaks Unite" that came with "Skull & Roses" in 1971 and the request to "send us your

Bill Walton appeared with Mickey Hart at ARCO Arena on February 9, 2011, before the Sacramento Kings took on the Dallas Mavericks.
© 2011 NBAE. Photo by Rocky Widner/NBAE via Getty Images

stuff" amid the proclamation that "we'll keep you informed," nobody had any idea what the last station on this line might be. In those innocent days of infancy it was Mary Ann Mayer handling the mail that started as a trickle but soon swelled to a spring flood runoff that required the help that showed up in the angelic grace and classic beauty of Eileen Law.

From that early pairing came the first Grateful Dead newsletter and the Hotline, with Eileen's calm, reassuring, closing tone and tune, "Thank you, and stay in touch."

Ticket sales then were "at the door," through Ticketmaster, or at the local record stores.

But with the ever-growing and changing demographics of the audience, Eileen and Mary Ann could soon barely keep up with the mail that flowed to P.O. Box 1065, San Rafael, California, as they steadily built the proudly confidential and ever-important mailing list.

As with all things Grateful Dead, inspiration moves us brightly. So it was in the early 1980s that Danny Rifkin, as true a saint of circumstance that has ever lived, came up with yet another totally unique vision of the band staying pure to its mission of being wholly self-contained. This dream conjured the Grateful Dead selling their own concert tickets through their newly created entity, GDTS— Grateful Dead Ticket Sales.

One of the many powerful mantras of the Grateful Dead over the years has been, "We do what we want." And one of the real benefits of being in the Grateful Dead was that you got to hire your friends and family members for what turned out to be not only the coolest of jobs but the most important ones as well.

When Danny Rifkin, Rock Scully, and Alan Trist were sifting through the dizzying numbers of applicants for the head of the GDTS force, and with the fate of the known world in the balance, in walked the recently unemployed Steven Marcus. Steven was and is a Dead Head. Steven desperately wanted and needed this dream job, but the process and interviews were tangibly difficult and painful. Steven was thinking to himself that it wasn't that long ago that he was completely shut out of his own miracle ticket, sitting and fretting in the parking lot on October 10, 1982, at the Dead show at Frost Amphitheatre at Stanford University—unable to even get in the gate. And now here he was interviewing for the job that would put him in charge of *all* the tickets.

When the inevitable question came to Steven about what happened with his last job and why he didn't have one now, he shyly responded that he had been fired from his previous job as an assistant to a concert promoter because he was regularly complaining about the overselling of the house. Danny, Rock, and Alan immediately pounced on *that* and barked in unison, "YOU'RE HIRED."

And so it all began. What started as a day-to-day existence for Marcus that Rifkin figured might last six weeks just kept rolling away and ultimately became just like the music itself—it never stopped.

There was no advertising for any of this, just word of mouth and the Grateful Dead Hotline. At the beginning of GDTS in March of 1983—literally a dawn of its own new era of communication—things started slowly. The first "office space" was Billy Grillo's cool apartment next to the Front Street studios and clubhouse. Steven was eventually joined by Calico and Frankie Accardi as the volume swelled. While they worked, they could hear the band rehearse through the walls. They stored everything in The Vault next to all the treasured racks of the recorded music.

Momentum started to build rather quickly, and it was tough to decide whether everything was getting better and better or worse and worse.

Shows and tours were announced on the Grateful Dead Hotline, generally a couple of months in advance. When the 1983 New Year's Eve show was announced, Steven, Calico, and Frankie were overwhelmed, as if standing before

the flood. There were more than 40,000 requests for the 9,000 tickets available for the San Francisco Civic Auditorium. The dream had come true. Figuring that this phenomenon had legs and was built to last, the decision was made to go for some real space, so GDTS moved into the upstairs unit above Camille's Travel Agency across the street from the Grateful Dead offices at 5th and Lincoln in San Rafael. Despite the fact that the number was never publicized, the phone never stopped ringing.

Grateful Dead Ticket Sales only had access to about a third of the total number of available tickets. The number of tickets sold over the years grew at a phenomenal rate, from more than 24,000 in the first year (1983), which really spanned only about six months, to being on pace to far surpass 700,000 in the last year before everything changed forever in August of 1995.

The challenge for all fans became how to distinguish yourself so that you became one of the chosen few from the tsunami of requests. Typically for a show that might have 15,000 seats, more than 60,000 requests would show up at the door.

Dead Letters, which opens with a letter from the Dead, is the story of shining the light on why you should make the cut and be allowed to play. Grushkin creatively begins with a copy of a beautifully handwritten, three-page explanation of a lot of things by Jerry Garcia. It's a personal response to an inquisitive fan letter from Craig Corwin in Fair Oaks, California, sent to the band in January 1967. The return address on Jerry's plain, white envelope simply says, THE DEAD. Its closing reads "Gratefully, Jerry Garcia (Cap'n Trips)."

And then the show and ride take off on a cultural, historic, and artistic time machine road trip through the galaxies as only Grushkin can orchestrate and navigate.

Eileen, Nadine Kaplan, and Diane Geoppo, along with Steve, Calico, Frankie, Joanne, and Carol at GDTS, saved the best of the best of the generous offerings that came to the Grateful Dead in meticulous and chronological order, carefully

THERE IS NOTHING LIKE A Grateful Dead CONCERT

protected in cardboard boxes at first and then ultimately in filing cabinets.

Today, there are more than 15,000 of these preserved envelopes that are decorated, painted, inscribed, and drawn, out of the countless millions that were submitted in search of the ever-elusive miracle ticket. Those 15,000 select gems are currently stored in the Grateful Dead Archive, safe and secure in the libraries at University of California, Santa Cruz, where Grushkin had unfettered access for this current work of genius. The artwork on the envelopes is incredible. With staggering imagination and creativity, the Dead Heads have interpreted the life and times of their heroes, songs, and friends. Page after page of the most remarkable art, in conjunction with Grushkin's painstakingly researched text, takes even the most experienced travelers to unimagined and previously unknown and unreachable destinations and elevations.

As you ponder the beauty, the hard work, the effort, the precision, the accuracy, the spirit, the time, the love, the desire, the interpretation, and everything else that has gone into all of this, never forget what was at stake. Was a complete stranger, a full-on Dead Head, who couldn't be fooled or tricked, who had seen so much, who was right in the middle of it all, going to notice *you*—and then make your dream come true?

And all of this art is done completely by hand. No computers, no technology, no ability to go back for a makeover. And all on Dead line and time. One time, one chance, and everything—all driven by sheer panic—all having to be better than perfect.

A good thing in and for the process was that all the people making the decisions were Dead Heads themselves; and they all had had their own personal nightmares of just how tough it was to get these cherished tickets. So when the Dead Heads would interpret the songs, the logos, the commercial art, the album covers, and anything and everything else to try to honor and appease the ticket gods, there was always the sense of myth and mysticism that accompanied their symbolic pleas.

The animals, nature, the storylines and storyboards, the figurines, the hieroglyphics, the serpents, the skeletons, skulls and roses, the sacred scrolls and language, the subliminal messages— they're all here, all with the Grateful Dead as the center of the universe. The way it should be. The way it is.

The freeform, collagist art that took creative, playful license in rearranging in mash-up style the vivid imagery of the Grateful Dead is not professional in that it was not done for silver. No, it's better than that, because it's done for life—the life that could only be had by getting a ticket into the show.

This in no way diminishes the spectacular quality of these one-time pieces of art—one-time in that there was never the slightest chance of any of it ever coming back.

Imagine what the postman thought as he would deliver truckloads of this stuff every day.

There was even discussion that it might be best to wear gloves in handling some of these precious jewels.

The band members themselves were very aware of all this. Steven, Frankie, and the staff would regularly post the best of the recent crop on The Wall, a 20x10-foot display museum board outside Steven's office. Grushkin has this photographic evidence as well. The guys would come by GDTS for a dose of inspiration and affirmation. It gave them a reason to believe in everything they were doing, including the special ability to see beauty in a sad world. Both sides of this master equation were fully aware of how much the fans drove everything and how meaningful all the feedback was.

The best part of it all—besides that it was saved for us today—was that it worked.

When you witness the magic of *Dead Letters*, your awestruck reaction will undoubtedly be the same as the people who first saw it decades ago.

"How can we *not* let these people in?"

The fans' reward for showing and sharing their heart was their ticket. This is your entry to the Promised Land.

Dream on, and enjoy the ride.

Dead Letters is essentially a love story—letters and all.

It's also living history that the eternal flame from the stage has now spread to the floor.

And for those of us who are Dead to the core, we know our love will be forever more.

Bill Walton

Preface

Gratefully, Cap'n Trips

In the case of the Grateful Dead—as with any tremendously popular rock 'n' roll band—the flow of fan–band love borne by the U.S. Postal Service was decidedly tilted from fan toward band. No way did anyone in the band have the time to reply directly to fan letters—especially not in the volumes in which they were arriving at band headquarters.

In fact, it wasn't long after the band's 1965 formation that Jerry Garcia could no longer respond directly to inquiries. For the one shining moment illustrated here, however, Garcia did offer a personal response to a query, in this case from a Sacramento fan named Craig Corwin who had just seen them perform at the Beaux Arts Ball.

In 1966 the Grateful Dead ventured out of the San Francisco Bay Area only a few times. The first was in February and March, when the band briefly resided in Los Angeles, playing obscure gigs and Acid Tests at the Northridge Unitarian Church, Compton's Youth Opportunities Center,

the A.I.A.A. Hall, the Danish Center, and the Trouper's Club.

The Dead did not adapt well to Los Angeles and, upon returning to the Bay Area, found a rental at Rancho Olompali in Marin for the summer. In July 1966 they ventured to Vancouver, British Columbia, for several nights at the PNE Garden Auditorium, but it wasn't until December 28 that they played their first non–Bay Area spot gig, at Governor's Hall in Sacramento (the Beaux Arts Ball).

There Craig Corwin saw the Dead for the first time, and he had a few questions for Garcia. He found the band by postal mail, likely at 710 Ashbury Street in San Francisco where the Dead had just established home base for the next eighteen months or so.

Corwin wanted to know about the songs the Dead played in Sacramento and about the guys. Garcia responded in kind, although looking back, historians like Dennis McNally and Nick Meriwether, along with the Dead's literary friend, Alan Trist, believe the information Garcia shared

was the "schtick" he was then using to explain the band's background to the press.

For whatever reason—likely he had a few minutes to spare—Garcia took the time to respond, in his own inimitable hand, focusing on a particular blues song Corwin had been captivated by: Reverend Gary Davis' "Death Don't Have No Mercy." It was one of the first songs that got an extended improvisatory treatment that evolved into dark jams (see also "Viola Lee Blues").

Garcia signed his letter "Cap'n Trips." In another month, that would not be seen again (Garcia rapidly came to dislike the bestowed moniker), forever replaced by Garcia's traditional "Yer Pal" signoff to all his correspondence.

In this one instance, however, Garcia offered a fan an extraordinarily thoughtful and personal reply. What a rare and tremendous piece, then, with which to kick off a celebration of what is perhaps the greatest love affair between band and fans ever charted in the annals of rock music.

DEAR CRAIG

THANK you For writing we appreciate such
EFFORT. I'm SORRY I haven't got around To answer=
ing BEFORE NOW, BUT you know.

The "DEATH song That you heard we sing is a
REV. GARY DAVIS song CALLED "DEATH DON'T
HAVE NO MERCY" OUR ARRANGEMENT ~~is~~ is
a somewhat updated version, but retains a
CERTAIN amount of The Feeling & The Tonality of
The original. I make no attempt To
duplicate DAVIS' Phrasing or melodic Lines
in The vocal. instead To just sing it more or
Less naturally. in Terms of our philosophical
atiTuDES Toward our music, we've carefully avoided
Forming Thoughts on The subject. The music says it all.
(Hopefully) most of our material is Traditional (at
Least The Lyrics) WE usually write our own melodies
and we always use our own arrangements.

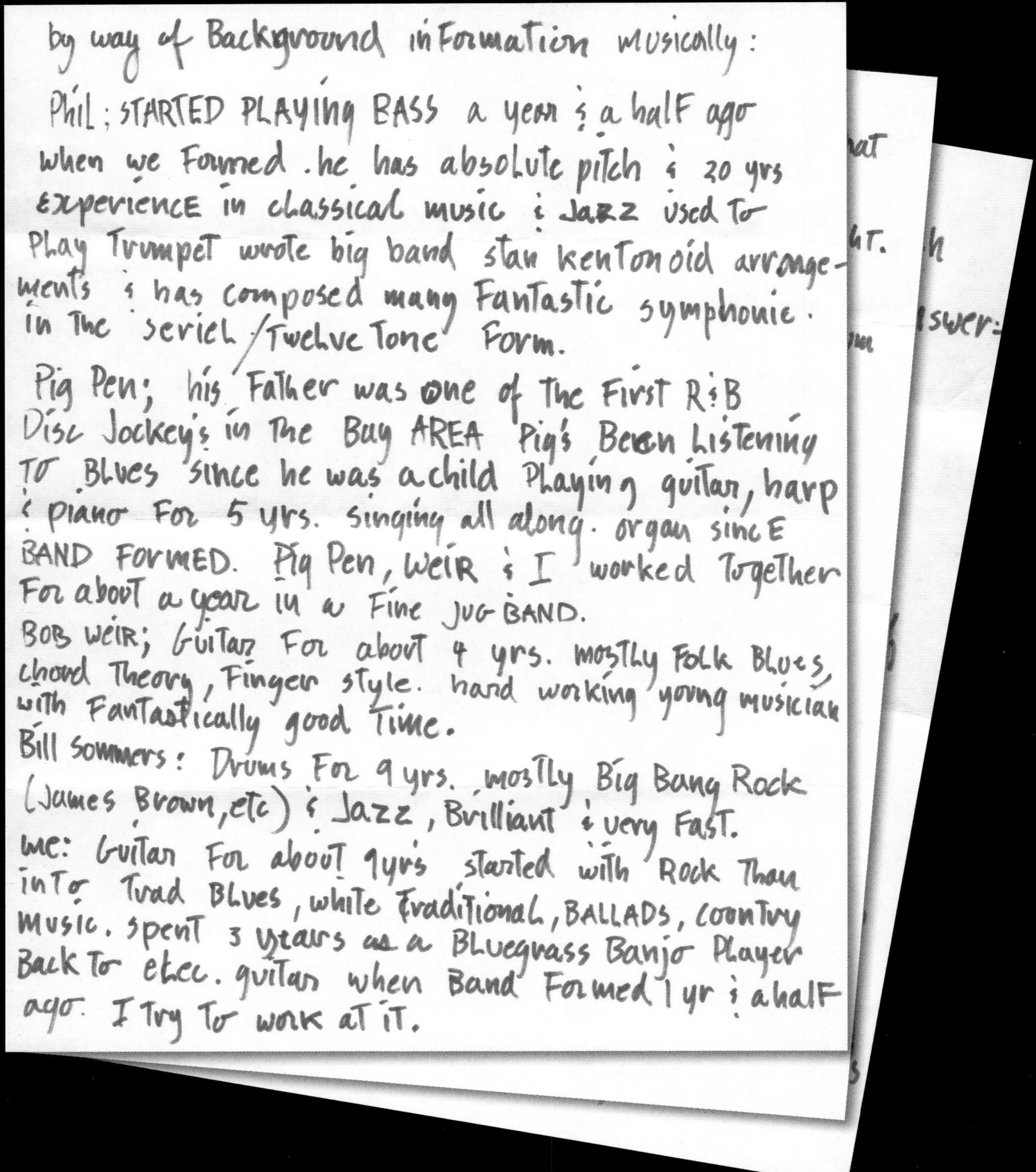

by way of Background information musically:

Phil; STARTED PLAYING BASS a year & a half ago
when we Formed. he has absolute pitch & 20 yrs
experience in classical music & JAZZ used To
Play Trumpet wrote big band stan kenTon oid arrangements & has composed many FanTastic symphonie.
in The seriel /Twelve Tone Form.

Pig Pen; his Father was one of The First R&B
Disc Jockey's in The Bay AREA Pig's Been Listening
To Blues since he was a child Playing guitar, harp
& piano For 5 yrs. singing all along. organ sincE
BAND FORMED. Pig Pen, WEIR & I worked Together
For about a year in a Fine JUG BAND.
BOB WEIR; GuiTar For about 4 yrs. mostly FolK Blues,
chord Theory, Finger style. hard working young musician
with FantasTically good Time.
Bill Sommers: Drums For 9 yrs. mostly Big Bang Rock
(James Brown, etc) & Jazz, Brilliant & very FasT.
ME: Guitar For about 9yrs started with Rock Than
into Trad Blues, white Traditional, BALLADS, coonTry
Music. spent 3 years as a BLuegrass Banjo Player
Back To elec. guitar when Band Formed 1 yr & a half
ago. I Try To work aT iT.

we like to play thats the big thing.

when we played in sacramento we felt that our performance was far below standard. I'm sorry you haven't heard us on a good night. We'll probably be back sometime,

we should be recording our first album within the next month, hopefully it will be out in 2 months. ~~warner~~ warner Bros.

Thank you again for writing:

GrateFully

Jerry Garcia

(Cap'n Trips)

PAGES 11–13: *Grateful Dead Productions. Craig Corwin collection*

Got a Letter This Morning

Dead Freaks Unite

Although Jerry Garcia hailed from San Francisco and Phil Lesh from the East Bay, in 1965 all members of the Grateful Dead (who had recently changed their name from the Warlocks) had become part of a growing new scene on the peninsula south of San Francisco, in and around Palo Alto. Their first compatriots, who included Ken Kesey and the Merry Pranksters, came from that locale as well. When the Dead briefly moved to Marin County in the summer of 1966, some fans followed, including Connie Bonner (now Mosley) and Sue Swanson (now Stallcup). They were among those gathered on May 22, 1966, for a legendary party thrown by the Dead at Rancho Olompali, a historic Mission-era adobe mansion on a hundred-acre property they were renting. That event set the tone for the band-fans relationship that followed.

That day, the Dead wanted to hang out in the sun-drenched California countryside, get high, get naked (as some of their friends did), and improvise music with fellow musicians from other major San Francisco bands like Quicksilver and the Jefferson Airplane. And that is the essence of what all Grateful Dead concerts forever afterward aspired to be: very loose, happy hangouts with people who appreciated the band's style of freeform music-making. To some small degree the gathering at Olompali also was the genesis of the original fan club.

ABOVE: The Grateful Dead party at Rancho Olompali presaged the more than 2,000 Grateful Dead concerts that would follow over the next thirty years. The band threw the party primarily for their fellow Bay Area musician friends in the summer of 1966. At that time the band's home was the adobe mansion at Rancho Olompali, a bucolic Mission-era estate in northern Marin County, a quite perfect setting for a legendary freak-out. *Artist unknown, photographed by Trevalyan Markle. Paul Getchell collection*

OPPOSITE: This unique Morroccan-influenced, fan-drawn postcard was sent to the band in 1975.

Pigpen (Ron McKernan), one of the band's founding members and a blues and R&B vocalist who also played keyboards, was the Dead's star attraction at the time, an immensely compelling character who by himself (the Dead backing him all the way) could take a concert to a whole new level. During the band's first years his soulful persona dwarfed that of all the other original members, even Jerry Garcia.

Connie and Sue both recall that the letters from original fans—people who were turning on to the band at the Fillmore Auditorium and the Avalon Ballroom (but in a general sense, really, grokking the entire San Francisco scene and not specifically the Dead . . . yet)—focused on Pigpen. "He got a *lot* of marriage proposals," remembers Connie.

Warner Bros. helped set up a rudimentary fan club by way of a brief note at the bottom of the back side of *The Grateful Dead*, the band's first album, released in 1967, by which time the band had shifted their home base to 710 Ashbury Street in San Francisco. A Pigpen look-alike contest was promoted in a few early issues of *Rolling Stone*, and Pigpen T-shirts were the band's first merchandise offering. Bill Graham even made Connie and Sue

wear tights and XL Pigpen shirts one night at the Fillmore—dancing on stage to draw attention to the merchandise table.

Back at her mom's kitchen table, Sue drew up the idea for a fan club poster. It would have a sign-in strip at the bottom, with a San Francisco post office box to mail it to. Sue then took her idea over to famed poster artists Alton Kelley and Stanley Mouse for execution in gold and green ink. A few hundred strips were returned fairly quickly, one from as far away as Nepal (with an enclosed piece of hashish).

Sue named the poster "The Golden Road (To Unlimited Devotion)," as her concept and their friendship with the band had just been rewarded with a song of the same name on the first album; forevermore the fantasy of the Golden Road would represent the fans' mythical destination. Later Kelley would recall it for the cover art of *The Book of the Dead Heads*. It also was the name chosen by Blair Jackson and Regan McMahon for their justly celebrated fanzine, *The Golden Road*.

Mouse and Kelley produced some of the band's first T-shirts by way of an innovative four-color-process technique invented by their own Monster

Company. But merchandising really took off when an array of T-shirts sold out instantly at Winterland Arena during a New Year's Eve 1971–1972 residency, prompting Bill Graham and Dell Furano to create Winterland Productions (which, in only a few years, would become the world's largest rock merchandising company). In the late 1980s, Grateful Dead Merchandising would be created to handle product development and distribution in-house, much in the spirit of how Grateful Dead Ticket Sales kept mail-order operations in-house.

In 1967 Connie and Sue, along with Bob Matthews, a longtime friend from Palo Alto who went on to mix sound for the Dead and co-produce some of their best albums, created the band's first newsletter, the *Olompali Sunday Times*, and mailed its amalgam of delicious tidbits to a list of about 150 people—friends and fans, but not yet quite "Dead Heads."

Fast forward to 1971. By this time there were five studio albums and two live albums. In the centerfold of the second live album, "Skull & Roses," there was a message from the band to their fans: "Dead Freaks Unite." By this time, the Dead's popularity had expanded far beyond San Francisco thanks to their appearances at college campuses throughout the nation and significant fan bases built in major cities like Chicago, St. Louis, Detroit, and New York. Garcia, songwriter Robert Hunter, the band members, and staff—notably Alan Trist, Jon McIntire, and Sam Cutler—wondered, "Who are you? Where are you? How are you?"

The famous Dead Heads mailing list evolved from the first responses to the "Dead Freaks Unite" message, correspondence directed to P.O. Box 1065

From the center spread of the "Skull & Roses" live album, in which the Grateful Dead reached out to its growing fan base by proclaiming "Dead Freaks Unite." The query marked the first time the Dead addressed their fans as Dead Heads. It also invited the reciprocal communication that would result in the creation of the band's legendary mailing list. © *Grateful Dead Productions*

TOP: After the initial deluge of correspondence that followed the "Dead Freaks Unite" message in 1971, Grateful Dead Records began receiving mail from around the globe. This envelope came all the way from Bahrain. *Steve Brown collection*

BOTTOM: Early on, the fan base figured the optimal way to contact band members was through P.O. Box 1065 in San Rafael—not that they'd expect an automatic or personal reply. This lovingly rendered Stealie is typical for 1974. *Steve Brown collection*

in San Rafael (a dedicated address for more than thirty-five years).

Initially administering that list was Mary Ann Mayer, a renaissance woman who did much of the artwork on the first mailings to the Dead Heads (including a stunning diagram of the 1973–1974 sound system affectionately known as the "Wall of Sound") and took most of the photos for the *Europe '72* album. Mayer also was a founding partner in the Heavy Water Light Show that backed Santana, the Dead, and others on dozens of nights at the Fillmore West. But Mayer personally was headed in an opposite direction; she joined a religious order and became a nun, moving completely away from the Grateful Dead scene by 1975.

But there was a young woman named Eileen Law about to step into Mayer's shoes and become the den mother to all Dead Heads for the next twenty-three years, until Garcia's death in 1995 and the cessation of the Grateful Dead as a touring phenomenon. She continued to be "head Dead Head" for another ten years until Grateful Dead Productions ceased. The archives she administered, along with the decorated ticket-request envelopes saved by GDTS, were donated by the band in 2008 to the University of California, Santa Cruz, where it all resides today.

Eileen—across the land she would be known by her first name—grew up in Guerneville, in Sonoma County, and attended many of the Dead's first San Francisco gigs (although, like so many others, she was really first a fan of the overall San Francisco scene). She and Rex Jackson, a member of the Dead's equipment crew, had a daughter, Cassidy, born at Bob Weir's house in 1970. Cassidy later became briefly involved with Grateful Dead Ticket Sales, but her major responsibility was assisting her mom with what had evolved into an enormous backstage guest list, one of rock's craziest ongoing scenes. (Jackson died in an automobile crash just after being promoted to road manager in 1976. The Dead named their charitable foundation after him.)

Eileen is the pivotal character in the band's interaction with its fan base. With Alan Trist from the Dead's songwriting company, Ice Nine, at the helm, and Mary Ann as co-producer, Eileen helped create the first newsletters and read *every piece of mail that came in*. The envelopes that came in were of every conceivable size and heft. Inside were poetry, mind-blowing artworks, photos, autograph requests, marriage proposals, Dear Abby–like dilemmas, love letters, lengthy ramblings about strange and unusual occurrences, and sadly, even a few death threats. As early as the fall of 1972, Eileen was determined to save the best of what was becoming one of the greatest outpourings of affection—as measured by the sheer volume of incoming correspondence—ever received by a rock band.

Much of the best correspondence comprised literally ten thousand attempts to describe

Mary Ann Mayer handled the graphics for the Grateful Dead's early 1970s newsletters and preceded Eileen Law as the Dead Head office manager. She was also a renowned light-show artist, frequently appearing at Bill Graham's Fillmore West with her colleagues under the name Heavy Water. Here she is shown in 1972 at an airport in Europe, surrounded by band members Bill Kreutzmann, Pigpen, and Phil Lesh (among others). *Photographer unknown, Eileen Law collection*

Now that we've got a moment to stand
what have we got
do we like it or not?
Kindly King of Light will explain the fine details
in the long run
but for the short run
the usual ambition, greed and just a touch
of goodwill
we put what faith we can muster there
not much and not often
but not Never, this far.
We build a way to get time
We build a way to grab on to chunks of it,
choke on it but would not spit it out
when so much effort has gone into getting
the damned thing half swallowed
(cf: Amoeba That Ate the World by Lefty Lamont)
One day perhaps all ambition will subside
leaving only eternity
pipers poets killers and men of state
in one drunken reel
given enough microphones of right impedence
we will record it
thanks for supporting us

© 1972 Ice-Nine Pub. Co.

the indescribable: how the Dead's musical improvisations had reached to the core of each fan personally. There was also general low-level griping about ticketing, seating, concert sound levels, difficulty in obtaining merchandise, and unseemly treatment of fans by concert promoters' staff—complaints that any successful rock band was likely to generate.

Eileen shared many of the most inspired (and concise) writings and artworks with the band members by pinning them to a bulletin board in the kitchen at the Dead's 5th and Lincoln headquarters in San Rafael, and it was a wonderful day when, say, Garcia would take notice of a particular submission.

Eileen's principal tasks as an employee were to process all the press clippings, maintain the band's album, CD, and DVD holdings, and attend to the Dead Head correspondence. She squirreled away all the best stuff in what initially was barely more than a large closet at the Dead's headquarters in downtown San Rafael. She was not charged with saving the best of the thousands of decorated ticket-request envelopes received by GDTS, but right from the beginning she worked in tandem with GDTS (which was just across the street) as she also coordinated the backstage-pass list that was an adjunct of ticket distribution.

To this day, Eileen says she just "knew in her soul" that the best of the correspondence had meaning and importance. Some of the first pieces she saved were featured in *The Book of the Dead Heads*, published in 1983, which the band solidly backed.

TOP LEFT: Eileen Law, longtime Dead Heads office manager, circa 1984, at the band's 5th and Lincoln headquarters in San Rafael, California. *Blair Jackson photo*, The Golden Road *fanzine*

BOTTOM LEFT: In 1972 and 1973 some of the most creative communications between the band and the fan base came in the form of the Grateful Dead newsletters. Complemented by Mary Ann Mayer illustrations, this poem likely was created by songwriter Robert Hunter and polished by Alan Trist, head of Ice Nine songwriting publishing. © *1972 Ice Nine Publishing Co., author collection*

In the field of promotions, Grateful Dead Records is particularly well remembered for the series of sampler EPs sent to the entire Dead Head mailing list. At some shows the band also set up a booth to further deliver the "Commercial Message," reinforced here by the signage of famed poster artist Alton Kelley and tie-dye hangings by Courtney Pollock. *Steve Brown collection*

From 1971 until 1983, only a small percentage of the envelopes in which the letters, stories, photos, and artworks arrived were decorated on the outside. When mail order became a major part of Dead Head life beginning in 1983, decorations on the envelopes themselves began to replace the earlier enclosed artwork. In many ways this was a fascinating development. Dead Heads now had a forum—the size 10 envelope—on which to share their love and knowledge of the band through the illustrations they created, even if, in effect, it begat what was in some cases an unsettling competition within the fan base for precious concert tickets.

The early newsletter mailings by the band featured upcoming tour dates, odd little cartoons by Garcia, notes on the Dead's latest equipment, flow charts explaining how the band's business operated, and meditations on success and its downfall. Perhaps most memorable were the ultracryptic "Hypnocracy" pages created by Robert Hunter, which purported to explain the philosophy of a mysterious St. Dilbert and thereby the inner workings of the Dead. Then, when the band began its own record company in 1973, Grateful Dead

Records, the newsletters became a conduit for information about new and upcoming releases.

The Dead Heads mailing list grew exponentially in the 1970s. At the time of the release of *Wake of the Flood* in 1973 (the first on Grateful Dead Records), the list had about 25,000 names. At that time the band had the resources to create sampler EPs and send them to everyone on the mailing list. By the time the label folded in 1976, the list had soared to more than 63,000 strong. Then, with the advent of Grateful Dead Merchandising and their creation of the content-rich *Almanac* mailer, the list doubled then tripled.

In the early 1980s, Eileen took on the task of inputting information into the band's official Hotline telephone banks, and Sue Swanson began converting the mailing list to a computer-friendly format. The Hotline became far and away the most efficient means ever of keeping Dead Heads informed. But the incoming mail never stopped, and in her archival mode (i.e., reading what the Dead Heads were talking or complaining about and saving the gems),

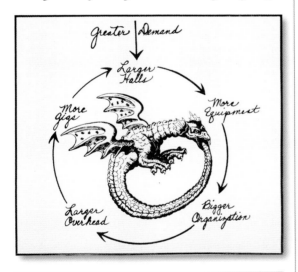

The "greater demand" graphic depicting a dragon chasing its tail was first published in one of the Grateful Dead's 1973 newsletters and subsequently reprinted in a seminal *Rolling Stone* magazine cover story entitled "Welcome to the World of the Corporate Dead."

Eileen was assisted by Nadine Kaplan (mid- to late '70s) and Diane Geoppo (1985–1995).

Meanwhile, the *Almanac* evolved into an enjoyable source of historical information, heads-ups on tours, and product promotions (announcing the latest wearables, recordings, and unique hard goods). When Grateful Dead Merchandising was merged into Rhino Records' operations at the time of the band's fortieth anniversary, the *Almanac* was not abandoned, though www.Dead.net soon became the key informational hangout and historical resource for Dead Heads (as it is today)—and Eileen was much involved, providing choice materials from "the stash."

A year before Garcia's passing, Eileen still was optimistic that the huge numbers of new fans could learn to appreciate what the Dead had long stood for. But as the 1990s began, there were unruly changes to the crowd structure, in large part because it was so vast and youthful and the band was now—god forbid, and like it or not—part of mainstream MTV-era culture. Thanks to their biggest hit single ever, "Touch of Grey," released in 1987, as well as the lure of adventure the band represented, the Dead were now in the same league as the Rolling Stones (i.e., among the top five largest grossing touring bands of the modern era). The parking lots at Grateful Dead concerts became destinations, and the band set attendance records everywhere they toured, from Madison Square Garden to Red Rocks Amphitheater.

"In 1972 we got the first mailing out to about 350 people," Eileen recalled in a 1984 interview with Blair Jackson for *The Golden Road*. "I thought then, well, that's the end of *that* job. Little did I know I'd still be at it more than twenty-five years later. . . . Even though it's gotten so much bigger, for the most part it still feels like a community. People continue to write us about births and deaths in their families, and we're starting to hear about Dead Head grandchildren. My sense is, as long as there's Grateful Dead music to be appreciated, there'll be Dead Heads doing that appreciating."

Today Eileen reflects, "My job was to keep in touch with people, listen to their concerns, and let the band know what I was seeing. All the while I was putting in a safe place the great stuff that I knew shouldn't be lost. Now with the archive having been given a new home at UC Santa Cruz, I've much hope that this slice of American rock 'n' roll life will be cared for properly and be accessible to students, scholars, Merry Pranksters, and of course, the Dead Heads."

Robert Hunter amused and confounded the Dead Heads by creating "Hypnocracy," an insider's interpretation of the Grateful Dead mythos, sent out into the world via the Grateful Dead newsletters in 1972 and 1973. *Author collection*

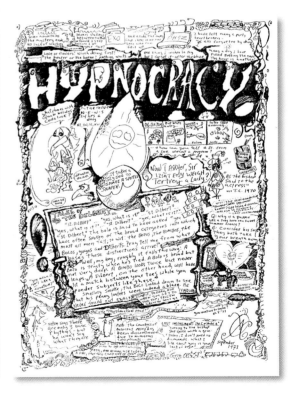

Grateful Dead: The Official Book of the Dead Heads

Dead Letters is the long-anticipated sequel to one of the most successful books ever created about the Grateful Dead: *Grateful Dead: The Official Book of the Dead Heads*. The former begins where the latter left off upon publication in 1983, the year the Dead began operating their own mail-order program that spurred the creation of tens of thousands of decorated ticket-request envelopes.

The Official Book of the Dead Heads received a significant honor when its Alton Kelley cover art was featured on the cover of *Publishers Weekly*, book publishing's industry journal, in January 1983. *Courtesy* Publishers Weekly

In the mid-1970s, I was living in a communal house in Portola Valley, in the hills west of Stanford University, with my brother, Jonas, a gifted photographer, and Jonas' then girlfriend, award-winning book designer Cynthia Bassett. We all were passionate, concert-going Dead Heads.

Post college, I was intermittently hanging with the Dead and staff at their 5th and Lincoln office in San Rafael, helping Eileen Law read the incoming Dead Head mail and thinking out loud about doing a book when a thought occurred to Jonas, Cynthia, and me: *"Let's tell the story of the Dead by way of the thousands of Grateful Dead T-shirts."*

Grateful Dead tees were beginning to establish a special identity all their own in pop culture, and the imagined book would be called *The Grateful Dead Book of Shirts*. It would have little or no text, letting the shirts tell the band's history and celebrate the close relationship the Dead enjoyed with the Dead Heads.

A mockup was created and even a few hilarious preliminary photo sessions were held. In early 1979 the proposal was presented to

Photo session for the proposed *Grateful Dead Book of Shirts*. Left to right are Jane Eskilson (wife of co-author Paul Grushkin), Cynthia Bassett (the book's designer and co-author), and Russ Stewart (family friend). *Jonas Grushkin photo*

the band members at one of their board meetings. "A great idea," everyone said at once, but then Jerry Garcia brought up the problem of trademark—if they allowed the *Book of Shirts* to proceed, the band would lose control over their merchandising trademarks.

There was a brief sad silence in the room until Garcia said, "Hell, they know all about us. Let 'em into our archives, and they'll make whatever book they see in there." Three years of arduous digging began—the first official use of the band's archives that primarily included thousands of press clippings and thousands of Dead Head letters, artworks, poems, and reminiscences

saved by Eileen Law and assistants Nadine Kaplan and Diane Geoppo.

Of course, the result was *The Official Book of the Dead Heads*, not the *Book of Shirts*. Compared to all the histories of specific bands published up to that point, none had ever been created as a journey through a fully fleshed-out (albeit imagined) concert. Every photo, story, poem, artwork, or newspaper account had to fit one aspect of the concert journey.

The Book of the Dead Heads remained in print for twenty-six years and went through sixteen American printings. Garcia wrote the foreword, and the book included the first-ever publication of the Dead's concert lists—a compendium later brought into prominence by the authors of Dead Base.

Famed poster artist Alton Kelley (now, sadly, deceased) created the all-new globe-in-skeletal-hand art for the cover, fleshing out the theme of "The Golden Road (To Unlimited Devotion)," a song on the Dead's first album.

When The Official Book of the Dead Heads was published, it became the first devoted to the Dead and their growing audience. The band and concert promoter Bill Graham received their copies backstage at the Berkeley Greek Theater on the last day of a glorious three-day series, May 13–15, 1983.

RIGHT: Alton Kelley's inspired Official Book of the Dead Heads cover art (a skeletal arm and hand holding a globe of the earth, with the Golden Road running from the foreground to the horizon) contributed a well-received new graphic to Grateful Dead iconography. For several years it was the basis for bold new licensed T-shirt art, including one popular variation showing the skeletal hand upholding "the Big Apple" to celebrate concerts in New York City. It also inspired artwork adorning several hundred ticket-request envelopes in the early 1980s.

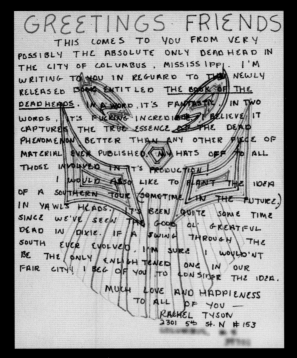

ABOVE: Co-authors Jonas Grushkin (left), Cynthia Bassett (center), and Paul Grushkin (right) celebrate with Grateful Dead: The Official Book of the Dead Heads cover artist (and pioneering concert poster artist) Alton Kelley in 1983. Photographer unknown, author collection

LEFT: Rachel Tyson, "possibly the absolute only Dead Head in the city of Columbus, Mississippi," sent this letter of appreciation to The Official Book of the Dead Heads co-authors. Author collection

21

Dear "Grateful Dead"!

Elnézésüket kérem amiért levelemmel zavarom Önöket.
Már nagyon régen nem hallottam az együttes zenéjét.-Still exist the Band?
Szeretnék kérni tájékoztatót.- I could supplicate prospectus?
Sok sikert kivánok!

Yours truly
            and
            thank you ever so much!

                    Name: Farkas György

                                    Hungarian

Dear Dead People,

Leafing through my American College Dictionary
and came upon a phrase, to wit:

"de Mortuis nil nisi bonum"

which translates:

"of the Dead say nothing but good"

I thought you might be interested in knowing
that the Ancient Romans appreciated good music.

Take care and
don't forget the milk

Anne K

"...Sun comin'up and then the sun it goin' down
shines Through my window and my friends they come around"

©Eyes Nine (LSD)

bye

Waiting
For
the Dead

SAGINA, CA 939
1 P.M.
31 MAY 1983

THIS SPREAD AND FOLLOWING: Correspondence with the Grateful Dead in the years prior to 1983 involved tens of thousands of fans pouring out their thoughts and sending them to the band via U.S. post. Often these letters and poems were accompanied by insightful photos and evocative artwork. Eileen Law's job at that time involved actually *opening* the mail, and she never failed to be surprised and elated when something tremendously wonderful tumbled out.

Yet, during those first dozen years—since the 1971 invitation urging Dead Heads to say something about themselves—fans rarely decorated their envelopes. In fact it was unusual to see a spectacularly executed Stealie beneath a return address or a watercolor of a bucolic scene pumping up the letter's destination: P.O. Box 1065 in San Rafael.

This was all to change in 1983, the year Grateful Dead mail order began in earnest. At first the ticket-seeking envelopes were plain or barely embellished. Then, some Dead Head unknown to this day figured out that full-blown decoration on that heat-seeking envelope might sway the ticket issuers. Thus the competition was set: Dead Heads would use all the imagination at their disposal to prove their loyalty, knowledge, and love . . . and by virtue of the most evocative envelopes ever sent in the mail, qualify for the greatest ongoing rock 'n' roll pay-in-advance sweepstakes ever known: winning *Grateful Dead* tickets.

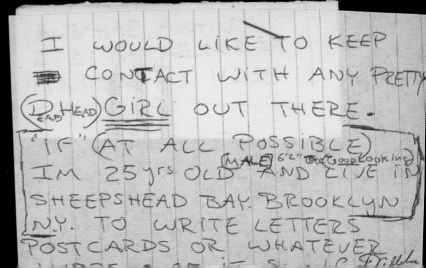

I WOULD LIKE TO KEEP CONTACT WITH ANY PRETTY (DEAD HEAD) GIRL OUT THERE. "IF" (AT ALL POSSIBLE) IM 25 yrs OLD (MALE 6'2" But Good Looking) AND LIVE IN SHEEPSHEAD BAY. BROOKLYN N.Y. TO WRITE LETTERS POSTCARDS OR WHATEVER

Thanks for being there at the Right Time.

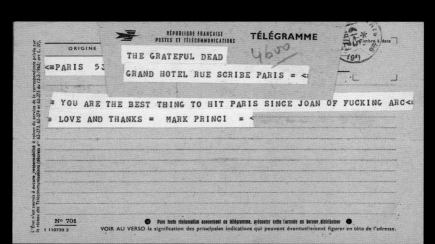

ORIGINE

<=PARIS 5

THE GRATEFUL DEAD

GRAND HOTEL RUE SCRIBE PARIS = <

= YOU ARE THE BEST THING TO HIT PARIS SINCE JOAN OF FUCKING ARC<=

= LOVE AND THANKS = MARK PRINCI = <

Nº 701

VOIR AU VERSO la signification des principales indications qui peuvent éventuellement figurer en tête de l'adresse.

GOOD OL' GRATEFUL DEAD

CHAPTER 2

Grateful Dead
Ticket Sales

(Please) Ease me in

At the peak of the band's success in the early 1990s, Grateful Dead Ticket Sales (GDTS) was moving half a million tickets a year by mail order, publicized only by the group's banks of sophisticated telephone hotlines on both coasts. At that point mail order accounted for one-third to one-half of all tickets the Dead sold annually (the rest were sold through conventional ticket outlets).

The Dead got into mail order for several reasons. They were concerned that they were not receiving the full measure of what they were due from conventional promotion, and there was evidence that some promoters oversold venues and did not provide proper accounting to the band. They were also concerned their fans were negatively affected by rising box office charges and by scalping. The band's main concern, however, was that the Dead Heads have the first shot at honestly priced, face-value tickets.

In 1968 the Dead and their fellow San Francisco–based psychedelic rock band, the Quicksilver Messenger Service, had promoted their own tour of the Pacific Northwest, giving them some initial ideas on how to independently sell and distribute tickets. But it was not until the Dead's fifteen-night fifteenth-anniversary run at the 2,000-seat Warfield Theater in San Francisco in 1980

ABOVE: Poster advertising the Grateful Dead and Quicksilver Messenger Service at Portland, Oregon's Crystal Ballroom as part of the 1968 Pacific Northwest Tour. For this tour the Dead handled the sale and distribution of tickets internally, a first for the band. *Art by George Hunter. Paul Getchell collection*

OPPOSITE: Superbly decorated envelopes helped Dead Heads score tickets—to a degree. GDTS staff was only human, after all, and humble but heartfelt envelopes sometimes met with as much success as the more stunning examples received. This R. Crumb-inspired piece would clearly fall in the latter category.

TOP: GDTS co-manager Steven Marcus at GDTS headquarters, posing for a *Golden Road* fanzine story, circa 1993. *Jay Blakesberg*

BOTTOM: Steven Marcus presides at the Grateful Dead ticket verification booth, Palace of Auburn Hills, Michigan, 1994. Ticket verification helped cut down on bootleg tickets and widespread scamming that targeted the band's legit mail-order services. *Photographer unknown, Steven Marcus collection*

that they began to see the full value of mail order. Bill Graham Presents ran a full-page ad in the *San Francisco Chronicle* that nowhere mentioned the name of the band but showed two skeletons holding a banner with Graham's famous quote, "They're not the best at what they do, they're the only ones that do what they do." The shows sold out speedily, and the mail-order portion of their ticketing held up well.

Fast forward three years. Eddie Washington (who produced the Garcia-directed *Grateful Dead Movie* [1977] about the October 1974 five-show residency at Winterland Arena) was hired to set up a mail order operation for three benefit shows in March 1983, also at the Warfield, as a fully in-house experiment. Washington called upon Steven Marcus, who'd worked on the fifteen-night anniversary run and was then an employee of Bay Area Seating Service (BASS).

Marcus had joined BASS in 1975. Over several decades, he became a master in revealing counterfeit tickets. During his dozen years as co-head of GDTS, he was responsible, along with the ticket-printing companies of Weldon, Williams & Lick, and Quicktick, for initiating and continually developing the Dead's elaborately designed tickets (complete with unusual colors, difficult-to-print sparkles, and occasional secret messages readable only under black light).

The band's oversize New Year's tickets had all manner of tricky aspects built in, successfully frustrating what were by then mad-dog counterfeit operations. Marcus also set up ticket-verification booths at concerts to spot fraud and alert ticket takers at the door to what the bogus tickets looked like.

The band's desire was that their hardcore fans, the Dead Heads, who'd been growing as a fervent, loyal base across the country since the early 1970s, would have first and easiest access to tickets through mail order. This was achieved with the second Warfield run. The band, in the person of manager Danny Rifkin, asked Washington and Marcus to do it again, although Washington left shortly thereafter

to resume his day job. Not long afterward, once the full concept of mail order was established, Rifkin selected Francine "Frankie" Accardi-Peri as co-manager with Marcus. Accardi-Peri would hire many key supervisors.

Some of the next shows with mail-order offerings included Stanford's Frost Amphitheater, Berkeley's Greek Theater, and a Santa Fe, New Mexico, gig. That year, 1983, GDTS sold 24,000 tickets by way of the now-famous first Hotline phone bank, which then comprised ten Code-A-Phones with a long message full of instructions for the fans.

The following year, 1984, GDTS sold 115,000 tickets by mail order, a healthy percentage of all the shows on all the tours. Yet, no more than fifty percent of all the available tickets were moved to mail order; the rest were sold through BASS,

These tickets for the Dead's 1983 three-concert benefit series at the Warfield Theatre in San Francisco were created specifically for mail order and represented the band's first serious attempt to solicit and process ticket requests. *Steven Marcus collection*

Ticketmaster, or Ticketron for a reason: to ensure that tickets would be available through all types of outlets. Only the New Year's runs of shows were considered for 100 percent mail-order fulfillment.

Looking back, in an interview with *The Golden Road* fanzine, Marcus observed that "everyone has the same chance to go to Ticketmaster as anyone else. There's an ad in the paper, you get in line, and you have a chance. Those tickets represent only half the house, but those are also half of all the good seats. Our main concern with Ticketmaster and similar ticket agencies was that unscrupulous ticket sellers within might be pulling off tickets for themselves or providing them to scalpers.

"Even if everything ran correctly," continued Marcus, "there were complaints. 'I waited in line for hours, I was the first person in line, and I'm in the 50th row?' Well, when you have a hundred outlets for a particular local show and a hundred charge-by-phones all going at the same time, and each one is capable of doing eight tickets a second, a thousand tickets can be gone in the first minute. So, mail order was the smart and viable supplement. It helped to even things out, to provide an equally fair chance at half the house."

No other major rock band before or since ever operated such an intensive mail-order business. And,

by extension, no other band received millions and millions of decorated ticket-request envelopes, all reflecting upon the band's unique ethos, of which 15,000 are now preserved at the Dead's archive at University of California, Santa Cruz.

At some point in the first year, a GDTS comment was printed in the mail-order instructions thanking the Dead Heads for decorating the envelopes that bore the money orders, providing visual entertainment for the ticketing staff. One wall at the GDTS office became a sort of hall of fame for the best envelopes. The Dead Heads quickly got the impression that decoration counted in a very important way—that the best decorated envelopes would be the first ones pulled from the bags and trays of received mail and be opened first.

They surmised that decoration would show the envelope pullers that a particular mail-order customer in fact was the *most truly dedicated*, the *most knowledgeable of Dead lore*, the *most loving to the nth degree*, and by his/her own self-reckoning the *most inspired fan* with the most pure, holy, and burning desire to attend a particular show or run of shows.

Decoration worked, but only to a degree. The GDTS staff was as human as the Dead Heads, and it would be very hard for any human being not to be impressed by a superbly illustrated (or humbly

TOP: Steven Marcus and Frankie Accardi-Peri at GDTS headquarters, San Rafael, circa 1987. This picture was taken in front of the famous "Wall of Fame." *Photographer unknown, GDTS TOO collection*

BOTTOM: The two GDTS headquarters houses in San Rafael, circa 1993. Both stories of the center building were utilized when mail-order operation was at its peak, employing as many as forty people to process a tour. *Photographer unknown, GDTS TOO collection*

LEFT: Dead Heads would do *anything* to score precious concert tickets, including humorous—and indeed shameless—sucking up to GDTS management! *Steven Marcus collection*

illustrated but just as heartfelt) envelope. But consider that in the last five years of the Grateful Dead their popularity was such that some shows received 60,000 ticket requests for a 15,000-seat venue. Those unrequited fans would have to take their chances with Ticketmaster or a scalper, find friends with extras, or pray for a miracle that if they showed up and waited outside the venue, someone—yes, it was known to happen—would walk up and hand them a ticket.

The mantra at GDTS was that if a Dead Head sent in a request by mail order and his order was one of the first envelopes picked, he should have a shot at seats in the first rows, just as—if that same fan stood in line at Ticketron and put down his money first—he should have a shot at the best seats in that other half of the house.

The point was to be fair, all things being equal, but with the band's popularity soaring, what was fair? So, GDTS took other measures to ensure various forms of fairness. Locally postmarked envelopes took some necessary precedence so, for example, a Landover, Maryland, show would not be populated by just New Jersey and New York Dead Heads, known for their particular zeal in scoring tickets. For another, if there was a run of shows involved, a fan shouldn't receive tickets for the same seats each night. Thus, each of the mail-order ticketers had piles of really good seats, good seats, and not-as-good seats. For the most part the overall response

---

TOP: GDTS supervisor Calico Van Der Mei prepares to honor mail-order ticket requests at GDTS headquarters, circa 1993. *Photographer unknown, GDTS TOO collection*

MIDDLE: GDTS supervisor Carol Latvala, circa 1993, in front of filing cabinets holding thousands of Dead Head informational 3x5 cards used in the GDTS postal-tracking process. *Photographer unknown, GDTS TOO collection*

BOTTOM: GDTS supervisor Joanne Wishnoff—top customer service specialist—in front of the Wall of Fame at GDTS headquarters, circa 1993. *Photographer unknown, GDTS TOO collection*

from the fans was, "At least I got in" or, "At least I got good seats to *one* of the shows."

The band achieved its incredible zenith of popularity in the early 1990s, becoming one of the top-grossing touring bands in the world, setting attendance records at prestigious venues across the country. This popularity followed the release of their most successful single, "Touch of Grey," in 1987, along with the Day of the Dead promotion on MTV that year. Steven Marcus remembers vividly that, seemingly, every third video shown on MTV that day was Grateful Dead–related, interspersed with cut-ins from the New Jersey Meadowlands parking lot showing "what a great scene it is out here, outside Giants Stadium!" For the first time, the parking lot scene became as important as the concert itself.

Soon the number of people in the parking lots doubled, then tripled. The result? The Dead broke into the American pop-music mainstream, which very likely was not their intention. Marcus reflected, "When I first started working for the Dead in 1983, the median age of our audience was about twenty-five to twenty-seven. Beginning in '87 and '88, the median age dropped to nearly seventeen. Everyone in the stands now was *so young*, but not necessarily attuned to what the Dead actually represented. Within weeks the demand for tickets was beyond enormous—it was literally painful for us to deal with. Now it would take a staff of sometimes forty dedicated people, all on the Dead's payroll, to complete the mail-order aspect for a run of shows or a lengthy tour."

Yet, GDTS was a great place to work. Everyone got free tickets and backstage passes to virtually every show (except reserved-seat fundraisers) and the tour bonuses sometimes exceeded what people were paid aggregately for working on the tour. Plus, there were Christmas bonuses, medical and dental benefits, and vacation pay.

But toward the end of the Dead's phenomenal run of success (before Garcia passed away in 1995, which brought an end to the name Grateful Dead as a touring entity), Marcus was compelled to advise

Song Interpretations

It Speaks of a Life That Passes Like Dew

Many Impressive statistics about the Grateful Dead and the hundreds of songs they played over the course of thirty years can be gleaned from the compendium of all compendiums, *Dead Base 10* (1997):

2,318 shows

36,504 songs played in all the concerts

480 different songs trotted out over time

What these numbers show is that an envelope-illustrating Dead Head had a *lot* of choices to make if picking a song to illustrate a ticket-request envelope. Dead Heads were further aware of the figures to the right, which indicate the number of times songs were played over the band's long career. The list is not indicative of a particular song's popularity among fans; rather, it reflects the band's whims—or inspiration. Some songs were downright evergreens, although the fervor with which any song was played in concert—again, on any given night—was what caused it to stand out and be particularly remembered:

1,265	"Drumz/Space"
613	"Me & My Uncle"
596	"Sugar Magnolia"
586	"The Other One"
581	"Playing in the Band"
552	"China Cat Sunflower"
549	"I Know You Rider"
549	"Not Fade Away"
520	"Truckin'"
475	"Jackstraw"
436	"New Minglewood Blues"
434	"Mexicali Blues"
433	"Tennessee Jed"
427	"Good Lovin'"
427	"Promised Land"
422	"Deal"
418	"Around and Around"
417	"Looks Like Rain"
397	"Big River"
393	"Bertha"
393	"Wharf Rat"
390	"Estimated Prophet"
388	"El Paso"
381	"Eyes of the World"
364	"Samson & Delilah"

"Turn on Your Lovelight" ranked thirtieth on the list; "Uncle John's Band," thirty-third; "Stella Blue," thirty-fifth; "Casey Jones," forty-first; "Terrapin Station," forty-fourth; "Walk Me Out in the Morning Dew," fiftieth; and "Dark Star," sixtieth.

Yet, all these impressive numbers mean little with respect to the decorated envelopes in this chapter. In the world of the Grateful Dead and the Dead Heads, it was all about *why did you choose this one song?*

OPPOSITE: Dead Heads often interpreted song lyrics in their drawings. In this category of envelopes, the Golden Road was one of the most popular images rendered.

That on-the-spot decision-making is at the core of why Dead Head ticket-request envelopes have so much "special" about them, and that's particularly true in this chapter because the envelopes here link the band and the fans in a unique way: as these envelopes illustrate (literally), both the band and fans interpreted songs and lyrics any which way they felt. There was only accounting for taste; relative popularity in and of itself had little meaning.

Because the Dead were an improvisatory band, *how well* each song was played on any given night, and in what sequence (what preceded each song and what followed afterward), was the subject of endless discussion and analysis. The experience of each song was the stuff of oral history, which parenthetically relates to the traditions of Native American storytelling. Native Americans ritually repeated myth-laden questions and answers. Dead Heads asked their

LEFT: This interpretive, decorated reel-to-reel tape box from the collection of legendary tape archivist Dick Latvala contains a concert's worth of music by Grateful Dead offshoot band Mickey Hart and the Hartbeats, recorded at the Matrix club, San Francisco, October 1968. Note reference to The Golden Road.

BOTTOM LEFT: Scarsdale, New York, High School student newspaper reporting on themes in Grateful Dead music following a 1976 concert run at New York City's Beacon Theater.

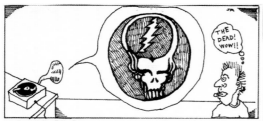

SHS 'Deadheads' Explain Their Mania

by Andy Friedland and Jay Lalezari

They're a band beyond description
Like Jehovah's favorite choir
People join in hand 'n' hand
While the music plays the band, Lord
They're settin' us on fire.

Tens of thousands of 'Deadheads,' followers of the rock band *The Grateful Dead*, made the pilgrimage to the Beacon Theatre in Manhattan on June 14 and 15, 1976, to fulfill a lifetime goal, but only a few thousand lucky ticketholders actually got in to see *The Grateful Dead* play. We were among them. Sitting among these drug-crazed people and listening to *The Grateful Dead* do their thing, we couldn't help but get swept away by the whole crazy thing.

The band — Jerry Garcia, Bob Weir, Phil Lesh, Keith and Donna Godchau, Billy Kreutzman and Mickey Hart — is a product of the 1960's, and is now a legend. To quote a *Grateful Dead* periodical, *Dead Relix*, published by a group of Deadheads, 'The Grateful Dead' represent many things to many people. For some they are the heads of some nebulous sort of collective messiah. Some think of them as a kind of collective messiah. Some think of them as musicians; some stopped thinking long ago and now simply feel. By and large, however, most people, when they consider the Dead, consider their lifestyle first and their music second.'

Conversely, many people enjoy their music long before they get into the Dead philosophy. But once they start relating to what the Dead are all about, they are hooked; there is no escaping. Even their music, superb before, now escalates to a whole new level of sound. But what are the Dead really all about?

Onstage and offstage, the Dead present a unique conception of how to live. They suggest simple ideas through their lyrics. One hero of the Dead philosophy is the rowdy cowboy who is always on the run.

Dallas, got a soft machine
Houston, too close to New Orleans,
New York's got the ways and mean
But just won't let you be.

Most of the cats that you meet on the street speak of true love,
Most of the time they're sitting and crying at home.
One of these days they know they gotta' get going.
Out of the door and down in the street all alone.

Also representative of this idea is the song about the gun-slinging cowboy of El Paso, who falls in love with a Mexican girl. After he kills a man over her, he is forced to run off to the ratlands of New Mexico. However, his love is strong and 'it pushes him onward back to the young maiden' where he is shot down by 500 cowboys.

A sharp contrast to the 'One More Saturday Night' cowboy image is the easy-going, loving feeling expressed in 'Sugar Magnolia.'

Sweet blossom come-on, under the willow
We can have high times if you'll abide.
We can discover the wonders of nature
Rolling in the bushes down by the riverside.
She's got everything delightful
She's got everything I need
Takes the wheel when I'm seeing double
Pays my ticket when I speed.

The themes go on and on. To grasp them all is up to you and your interpretation of what they mean. However, there is one basic and general idea which is being expressed continuously: live your life — live it to the fullest. Don't be selfish or obnoxious. Trust your feelings and care about other people. It can be a miserable world if you're not careful. All you have to do is want to laugh, be happy, and make the people around you happy too. This is a valuable concept to all of us here in Scarsdale!

Again we repeat, if these ideas are new to you and still very unclear — don't worry! It's no hassle, just spend some time listening to these good ol' boys. Get on the trail and one day you just might find the road. Until that time, if the feelings don't come right away and you start to wonder if these just aren't a bunch of crazy, acid freaks — relax — Jerry Garcia has an answer for you and it's really quite simple:

One watch by night
One watch by day,
If you get confused
Listen to the music play.

friends: *How did the song touch you? Which night did they play it best? Why did it sound so great? What did it make you think about? What memories did it bring back?*

Individual polling and nomination by consensus are equally inadequate tools by which to judge the full merits of Grateful Dead songs, because everybody's opinion counted equally and differently in some wonderfully helter-skelter fashion, kind of like judging a song by the rules of the Caucus Race in *Alice in Wonderland*. In fact the contributing numerology involved is simply staggering because the Dead never played the same songs in the same order, or in the same way, or with the same fervor and inspiration (or lack thereof) on any given night. At its best, Grateful Dead music was anti-formulaic. It had framework and was started anew, worked through, and finally completed more or less on the spot. No one musician really knew what suited the moment, so it had to be a spontaneous, collective decision.

For each involved, it was all about . . . *surprise!* Although to be fair, in the band's last few years, they'd arrived at some basic pattern with which to deliver

the experience. But that was not unexpected: it was hard to be 100 percent inventive every single evening. Though they tried. For the most part, given that they were the ultimate jam band, they did their best to reinterpret the experience, redefine the experience, channel the experience, and experience the experience as best they could. *It* wasn't always there, but on the nights it was, the Grateful Dead were like no other rock band. It's just that you weren't supposed to know in advance how it would turn out. Or which songs would be great, or which ones wouldn't.

So consider all this concert experience with respect to the ticket-request envelopes. Between the names of the songs themselves and then the lyrics, plus the history of the songs in concert and their initial release on albums, fans had an immense amount of material to work with when considering how to decorate their envelope. A Dead Head could focus on Jerry Garcia/Robert Hunter songs. Or Bob Weir/John Barlow material. Or the occasional Bobby Petersen contribution. Or who the Dead reinterpreted: Bob Dylan, Chuck Berry, Buddy

Holly, Johnny Cash, and any number of rhythm and bluesmen or just bluesmen. And let's not leave out pure folk music either.

A couplet might inspire an illustration or a favorite line. You can readily see the envelopes that were heartfelt creations for very personal reasons. But, turned on its head, an illustration created by a Dead Head might have just been rendered to impress upon the ticket issuers at Grateful Dead Ticket Sales that this person really *got it*—that they knew how to score with something deliciously obscure or decided it was best to turn in a really special graphic take on an old faithful. In the hands of the Dead Heads the choice was not simple: not everything was, say, "Sugar Magnolia."

Dead Heads had all the options available. A person could choose to illustrate a song that was among the most played by the band or one that wasn't at all high on that list. The choice of what to decorate with was in fact an element of what Dr. Seuss called taking things "on beyond zebra." Choosing a song or a lyric out of the myriad possibilities was an invitation to have at it and take it to some new place, just like the Dead did in concert.

In all the 15,000 envelopes saved at University of California, Santa Cruz, there appears to be some consensus on the most commonly illustrated songs (example: "Dark Star"). But in general it appears that Dead Heads just as many times chose songs that in some way touched their own lives (examples: "Attics of My Life" or "Black Peter"). And even if there was repetition with regard to certain chosen songs, no two illustrations examined any song, or any lyric, in the same way.

All of which means plumbing the Grateful Dead Archive's ticket-request envelopes for individual interpretations of songs and lyrics is its own psychedelic journey to the center of the universe . . . and so, on beyond zebra.

Ice Nine Publishing Co. response from Alan Trist (aka Bozo or Bokonan) to a term paper–related query about Grateful Dead music, 1973.

March 8, 1973

Richard L. Boyce
14689 160th Avenue
Grand Haven, Michigan
49417

Dear Rich,

Yes, indeed, the inspiration for the name of the Grateful Dead's publishing company (Ice Nine) comes from Vonnegut's "Cat's Cradle." The symbolism as we would see it, has more to do with mystic world-death, rather than physical world-death. This is a positive aspect, and reflects the cliff-hanger the world (planet) has come to (pollution of both the physical and moral orders); and the narrow line between enlightenment and world end.

An underlying theme of the Dead's music is precisely this narrow line; the need to walk it, and the difficulty of pinning it down. Another way of looking at the Ice Nine concept is in relation to the logo (above) which is a hexagram from the I Ching ("Gathering Together" changing to "Holding Together.")

Best of luck with your term paper.

Regards,

Bozo/Bokonan

AT/el

P.O. Box 1073, San Rafael, California 94901   Tel: (415) 457-1830

ABOVE: Dead Heads often decorated their ticket-request envelopes with dead-on accurate reproductions of the band's album covers by famous artists like Stanley Mouse, Alton Kelley, and Rick Griffin. However, this book includes only highly personal interpretations of that album art, such as this take on the back cover of *Europe '72*.

RIGHT: Artist: Christopher Wilson

BOTTOM LEFT: A Dead Head ticket-request envelope that illustrates the essence of Grateful Dead music, i.e., playing off the band's reputation as the world's leading jam band.

ABOVE: An example of a Grateful Dead lyrical conundrum as illustrated on a ticket-request envelope: The sky was yellow and the sun was blue from "Scarlet Begonias."

Grateful Dead
Ticket Sales
New Years Eve
Box C-S 8190
San Rafael, Ca.
94912

Here Comes
Sunshine

SOLDIER FIELD

WITH SONG

Grateful Dead Ticket Sales ~ New Years Eve
Box C-S 8190
San Rafael, California
94912

GO With The Flow

ITS ALL U NEED!

DEC. 31st ~ 2 tickets
PEACE! NEW YEARS EVE

...ANOTHER
SUNSHINE DAYDREAM!

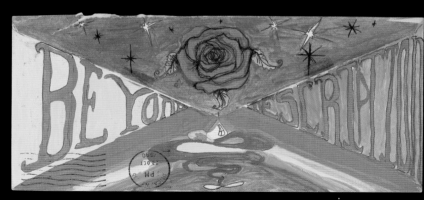

BEYOND DESCRIPTION

To: Grateful Dead Tix Sales
Box C-S 8190
San Rapheal CA
94912

N.Y.E.

"picture a bright blue ball just spinning, spinning free, dizzying with possibilities"

Shall we go, you + I while we can?

ST. STEPHEN WILL REMAIN: ALL HE LOST HE SHALL REGAIN

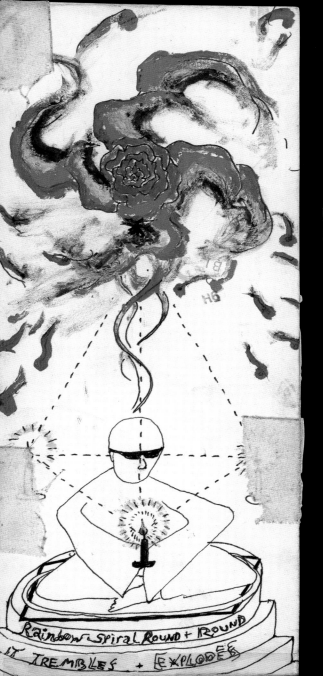

Rainbow Spiral Round + Round
It Trembles + Explodes

SUNSHINE!
DAYDREAM!

HEY NOW!!

COME BACK TO KINGSWOOD!

GRAB

GRATEFUL

MADE IN CANADA!

LUCY

The Stealie

What Shall We Say, Shall We Call It by a Name?

ABOVE: Grateful Dead amplifier road case with Jet Fuel and Stealie stickers. Frost Amphitheater, Stanford University, 1983. *Philip Grushkin photo*

OPPOSITE: The Grateful Dead's Stealie logo is easily one of the most recognizable in all of rock. Its success is due in no small measure to the fact that it's relatively easy to draw—though some folks, like Rob Sullivan, have offered more complicated and highly personalized visions of the Stealie over the years.

The Woodstock Music and Art Fair (August 15–18, 1969) was pivotal in more than one respect —it also marked the first sighting of the Grateful Dead's "lightning bolt" equipment-marking stencil, the immediate predecessor to the band's trademark skull-and-lightning-bolt "Stealie" logo.

The Stealie logo is today regarded as one of the five most instantly recognizable rock band graphics, along with those rendered for the Rolling Stones (*lips and tongue* by John Pasche, 1971); Yes (*flowing, linked letters* by Roger Dean, 1972); KISS (*comic-style letters* by Ace Frehley, 1973); and AC/DC (*beveled letters with lightning bolt* by Gerard Huerta, 1976).

The Grateful Dead song "He's Gone," from which the Stealie term was derived, debuted at the Tivoli Gardens in Copenhagen, Denmark, on April 17, 1972, during the first leg of the band's legendary Europe '72 tour (the song would first appear on the *Europe '72* live album). " The song includes the lyric:

> *Like I told you,*
> *What I said,*
> *Steal your face*
> *Right off your head.*

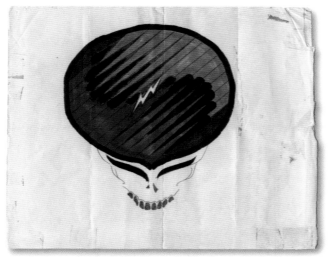

The full Stealie graphic work-up first appeared on an album as the small central focus on the front cover of *History of the Grateful Dead Vol. 1 (Bear's Choice)*, released in July 1973. The logo later was used as the full cover of the mostly unloved *Steal Your Face* live album released in June 1976 (featuring live material from the band's pre-"vacation" Winterland shows in October 1974), although ironically "He's Gone" does not appear on either album. Historically, the song was performed infrequently only to commemorate the passing of key figures, such as Northern Ireland protest hero Bobby Sands and the Dead's own Ron "Pigpen" McKernan.

But back to 1969 and one of the major contributions from Owsley "Bear" Stanley III (1935–2011), the inventor of the Dead's original traveling concert sound system. During the course of that year, the Dead seriously began playing festival-type events that led up to Woodstock and, in the following eighteen months, a great profusion of other festivals, including helping the Rolling Stones organize their doomed free concert at Altamont Speedway.

Bear explained on his Web site (www.thebear. org) the necessity of coming up with a visually striking graphic marker for the Dead's equipment cases: "The Dead in those days had to play in a lot of festival-style shows where the equipment would all wind up at the back of the stage in a muddle. Since every band used pretty much the same type of gear, everything looked alike. We would spend a fair amount of time moving the pieces around so we could read the name on the boxes. I decided we needed some sort of striking graphic that we could identify from a distance."

In 1969 the Dead had just moved back to Marin County from San Francisco, settling in Novato and renting a warehouse along with their pals at Alembic Sound near the shuttered Hamilton Air Force Base.

Bear lived in Oakland, across the Bay. Bob Thomas, an artist friend of both Bear and the Alembic crew, had just moved from Los Angeles to the Bay Area and needed a place to stay. The Dead needed someone to look after the warehouse with its sound equipment and instruments because of the threat of break-ins.

"I was in the habit of driving from Oakland to Novato in a little MG TF," continued Bear. "It had plastic side curtains which were not very transparent, due to the aging of the plastic. One day in the rain I looked out the side and saw [a building] next to the freeway that had a sign with a circle and a white bar across it—the top of the circle was orange and the bottom blue. I couldn't read the name of the firm but was struck by the shape. A thought occurred to me: if the orange was red and the bar were a lightning bolt cutting across at an angle between the red and the blue, then we would have a very nice, unique, and highly identifiable mark to put on our equipment."

Bob Thomas by that time had taken up residency on the mezzanine of the warehouse. "I told Bob the idea that I had," continued Bear, "and he made a quick, intuitive sketch, one that incorporated a thirteen-point lightning bolt. A mutual friend, Ernie Fischbach, who was visiting with Bob, said 'Give it to me, I'll show you an easy way to put it on the equipment cases,' whereupon Ernie proceeded to cut holes in a couple of pieces of stencil paper. One was a circular hole, about five and a half inches in diameter, and the other was a half circle five inches in diameter and with a jagged edge, like the bolt. Ernie held the stencil to an amp and sprayed a circle of white paint. Then with one side up, the red half circle went on top of the dried white paint. Ernie wiped the red paint off the stencil, turned it over, and applied the blue.

"So that was the very first version of the bolt-in-circle and we proceeded to stencil it on all our gear and cases. Not long thereafter we left on tour and made our way to Woodstock, and it did make it easier to find all our stuff in all that crunch."

Some time after, Bear and Thomas got to talking again. Bear suggested that perhaps the words "Grateful Dead" could be placed under the bolt-in-circle, using a style of lettering that would appear to be a skull if seen from a distance. When the lettering idea didn't quite work, Thomas came up with the compressed bottom half of a grinning skull that incorporated the red and blue circle with its bolt. *Voila!*

As early as 1969 at their Novato warehouse/rehearsal space/office, the Dead began using the full new design as their letterhead logo. In 1970 when they moved to their longtime office digs at 5th and Lincoln in San Rafael, the soon-to-be-termed "Stealie" skull logo was replaced by an adaptation of the older skeleton-head-and-roses design, which had first been drawn by psychedelic artists Stanley Mouse and Alton Kelley for their iconic September 1966 Avalon Ballroom Grateful Dead concert poster. Now the Grateful Dead had two trustworthy, highly recognizable logos that they formally trademarked in 1972.

But the Stealie was simply waiting for its own big stage, having swiftly become one of the world's most recognized rock band logos and merchandising anchors. In 1972 the Dead Heads began freely adapting the Stealie on their own as seen on the correspondence with the band that followed the October 1971 "Dead Freaks Unite" message in the gatefold of the "Skull & Roses" album.

Hundreds—then thousands—of letters and envelopes sent to P.O. Box

  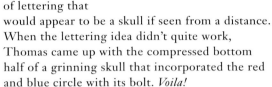

1065 incorporated, among the poems, photos, narratives, stories, and complaints, such unusual and imaginative re-created Stealies that the band and staff could do little but chortle upon receiving the bags of mail.

Since then, Dead Heads by the tens of thousands have reworked and reinterpreted the skull's features and applied myriad images to its dome (from marijuana leaves to the Golden Road to the Taijitu [yin yang], and everything conceivable and even seemingly inconceivable). In the process—*and this is key*—they have in effect individualized the mark.

Unusual for rock, the Dead became more and more comfortable with the process of fans' never-ending re-creations of the band's trademark symbology. Generating new and previously unimagined Stealies mirrored the band's own tradition of constantly reinterpreting their songs in concert. Just like there is no end to the number of Grateful Dead musical improvisations, there is no end to the number of improvised Stealies. This would seem to mean, "We are all in this together, but we are also all completely different."

P.O. Box 1073
San Rafael. Calif.
94901

TOP: Clever Dead Head interpretations of the Stealie have included a "3D" effect (left) and the replacement of the lightning bolt with a map of New Jersey (by Frank Brattole) and a cannabis leaf..

LEFT: Grateful Dead business envelope with Stealie logo, circa 1970, first used when the band was headquartered in Novato, California. *Eileen Law collection*

THIS PAGE: Over the years Barry Haden has created some of the most memorable Grateful Dead ticket-request envelopes (see pages 156–157). More than once he has bent the Stealie to his unique vision.

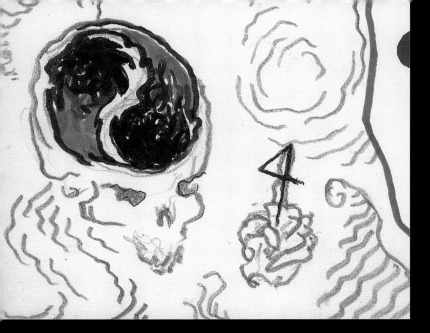

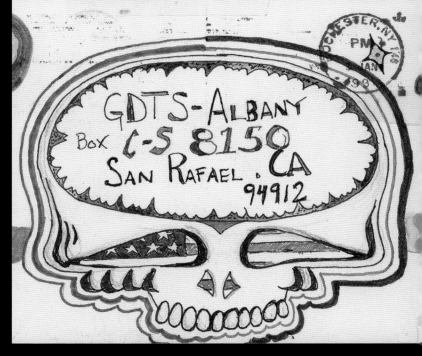

GDTS-ALBANY
Box C-S 8150
San Rafael . CA
94912

GRATEF
(NEW Yo
BO
SAN

Grateful Dead Merchandising created their first in-house Stealie, known as "Space Your Face," in response to the many Dead Head re-creations

G.D.T.S - NEW YEARS EVE.
C-S 8190.
SAN RAFAEL, CA 94912

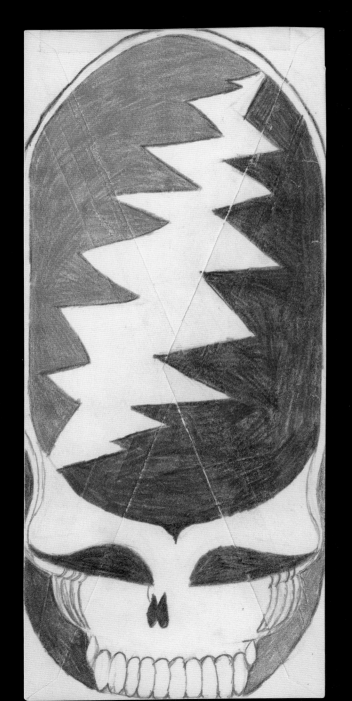

G.D.T.S - Atlanta, Ga (omni)
P.O. Box C - S 8190
San Rafael, Ca 94912

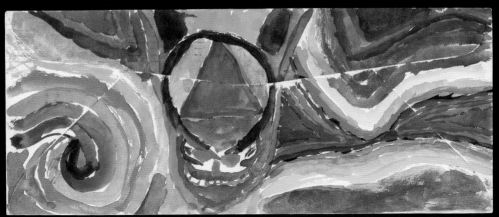

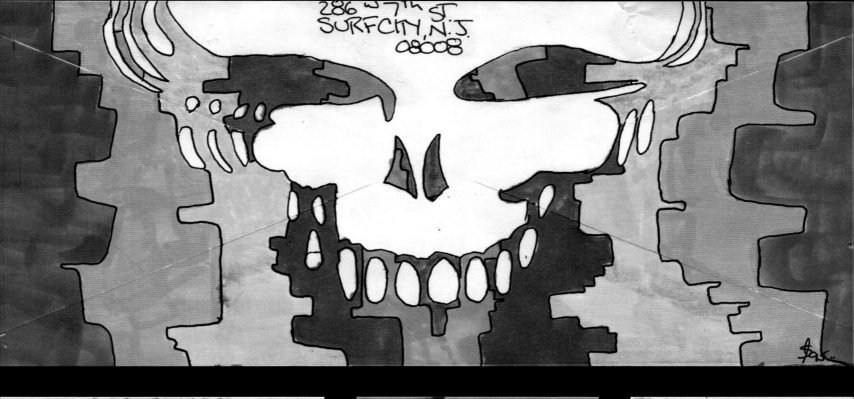

Grateful Dead Ticket Sales - Greek

Box C-S 8150
San Rafael Calif.
94912

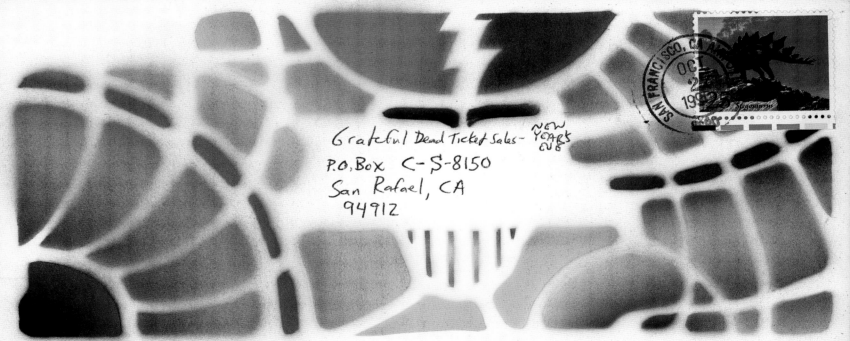

Grateful Dead Ticket Sales- NEW YEARS EVE
P.O. Box C-S-8150
San Rafael, CA
94912

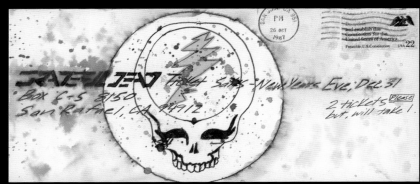

Grateful Dead Ticket Sales - Albany
Box ES 8150
San Rafael, CA 94912

Grateful Dead Ticket Sales - Frost
Box C-S 8190
San Rafael, CA 94912

2 Tickets For Each Show

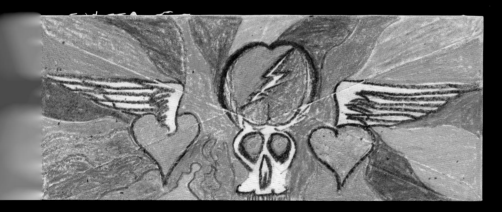

Grateful Dead Tickets
New Years Eve
P.O. Box C-S 8190
San Rafael CA
94912

29 USA

The Lightning Bolt

Arrows of Neon

Of the two official Grateful Dead graphic marks, the Stealie caught on the quickest. It appeared in every city and country around the globe where Dead Heads were found, and their correspondence with the band bears that out.

But the graphic from which it was originally derived—the white, thirteen-point lightning bolt in its red-and-blue round shell—had just as huge an appeal for the band's fans, appearing nearly as frequently as the Stealie on the envelopes and artworks they sent to the Dead's post office boxes (particularly the for-Dead-Heads-only P.O. Box 1065 in San Rafael, California).

The Stealie, which incorporated the lightning bolt in its skull dome, was freely reinterpreted, redrawn, and messed with by Dead Heads for more than forty years. By contrast, in that same time period, the lightning bolt retained its basic graphic integrity despite some occasional creative stretching and pulling.

The latter's success had to do with the ease with which it could, and did, appear in just about every conceivable context, as evidenced by the ticket-request envelopes. The lightning bolt was another enticing invitation to the Dead Heads to "have at it," and they put it into play as the centerpiece of a

million different vignettes, a symbol for any one of the seemingly gazillion aspects of the band's ethos.

Owsley "Bear" Stanley III and his colleague, graphic artist Bob Thomas (creator of the covers of *Live/Dead* and *History of the Grateful Dead, Vol. 1 (Bear's Choice)*, as well as co-creator of the Stealie) introduced the lightning bolt for a specific purpose—to mark the Dead's equipment cases—with the Stealie then resulting from the bolt (see the previous chapter). Stanley Mouse and Alton Kelley came up with the skeleton and roses mark (the basic theme appearing first on Family Dog poster #26 and later on the 1972 "Skull & Roses" album), but the Dead Heads were not long in adopting the lightning bolt as the unofficial third graphic mark.

The lightning bolt as a symbol of something very powerful actually tracks back to the dawn of man. Cavemen knew there were few displays so pure as the power of nature—a brilliant flash of blue-white light that seems to arc out of the heavens as if by magic, and the near deafening thunderclap that comes mere seconds later. Early man had many explanations for lightning and thunder, and the myths that evolved involved elaborate tales of gods and goddesses and mythological creatures who used lightning as weapons.

To the Greeks, lightning bolts were thrown by the hand of Zeus, the father of all gods and men, the ruler on Mount Olympus. The Romans saw lightning as the symbol of their Zeus equivalent, Jupiter. In Norse legend, Thor was the god of thunder and lightning bolts were the sparks that flew when his mighty war-hammer hit its target.

In many Asian cultures, sky dragons were responsible for lightning strikes that split trees and struck down unwary humans. Navajo myths linked lightning to the Thunderbird, the symbol of salvation and divine gifts. In modern times, stylized

OPPOSITE: Even easier to render than the Stealie among Grateful Dead iconography is the lightning bolt logo. This Dead Head ticket-seeker dressed it up with their take on the Dead's skeletons and skull and roses imagery (see following chapter).

lightning bolts evolved to symbolize the power and danger of electricity.

Because no one knew when lightning would strike, it symbolized the capricious nature of gods and the world men lived in. But because lightning often accompanied a rainstorm, it also was seen as a symbol of fertility and, in many cases, represented instant, divine, and positive intervention, a wake-up from a higher source (a message for the observer to open his eyes and pay immediate attention to his situation and surroundings).

As modern culture evolved, lightning also came to represent a stroke of genius, clarity of understanding, and sudden epiphany—the creative spark, which underscores its appeal to the Dead Heads. Its jolt is such that it represents intuition, spontaneity, and synchronicity, all important elements in Grateful Dead music.

The lightning bolt also represents what the band called the instant appearance of the "missing member" that binds everything together in one palpable step up—say at the beginning of a great second set. It represents the magical, unspoken combination of the band members' skills; their collective mental improvisations; their on-the-spot, newly created rendition of a flow of songs; the overall sharpened acuity of their presentation; and the passionate urging-on of an audience that is suddenly appreciating all the new developments.

For the Grateful Dead and the Dead Heads, what's key is that lightning can't be predicted or summoned into being. It's celestial power and spiritual illumination that's delivered in a sudden, unexpected realization of truth. Through the Grateful Dead's music, it's the momentary appearance of a higher reality at a Grateful Dead concert. This didn't happen every time, but it did happen so many times that both the band and the fans believed it when they saw it.

Thus, the lightning bolt—and that's a lot to lay on one unofficial symbol!

"Shazam" lightning bolt conceptual art by Barry Haden. *Courtesy Barry Haden*

Bob Thomas

Bob Thomas was truly a Renaissance man. Beyond his accomplishments for the Grateful Dead—as co-creator of the Stealie and the lightning bolt logos with Owsley "Bear" Stanley III and illustrator and designer of the cover art for the *Live/Dead (1969)* and *Bear's Choice* (1973) albums—Thomas was a world-class bagpipe player, restorer, and builder. He was cofounder of the eclectic Golden Toad, the "house band" at the Renaissance Pleasure Faires in southern and northern California (and an opening act for the Family Dog at the Great Highway).

Thomas was born in Hollywood in 1938. He attended the U.S. Navy School of Music, Georgetown University, UCLA, and the Art Center School of Los Angeles. He moved to Northern California in 1966 and met Bear in early 1969, falling in with the Grateful Dead scene that was newly coalescing in Marin County after the band's celebrated residency in San Francisco's Haight Ashbury.

Beyond the logo and album artworks, Thomas painted in psychedelic style one of the first Alembic custom boutique basses played by Phil Lesh. His Egyptian Eyes of Horus were seen for a time on Bill Kreutzmann's and Mickey Hart's drum heads. He also created Alembic's logo, and his psychedelic paintings still adorn the walls of the guitar-maker's factory in Santa Rosa.

Bear, on his Web site, www.thebear.org, noted his deep appreciation for the hallucinatory visions reflected in Thomas' art:

When you look at it, you think: This is strange, it seems sort of messy . . . but if you take acid and look at the painting again you see all these highly complex patterns melt into each other. . . . When you took psychedelics and gazed at his work, you would see these patterns. With any other normal painting the patterns would not come to the forefront. Bob knew how to "fix" the patterns so your mind would follow them each and every time. The Grateful Dead's music is also like that. There's stuff "painted" into it, in musical notes that create a psychedelic tapestry. Sometimes you don't detect the patterns when you're straight, but when you're high the Dead's patterns take you to another level, just as Bob did with his.

In his other, non–Grateful Dead life, Thomas was a renowned performer in folk and world music, highly skilled on the Macedonian, Portuguese, and Italian bagpipes. He also was adept on the lute, guitar, viola da gamba, and various shawms and flutes.

Sometimes his band, Golden Toad, was joined by as many as forty folk musicians on stage at a time, as at the annual Charles Dickens Christmas Faire in San Francisco. Thomas, according to one of his peers, "presented the act as a 2,000-year-old continuous entity stemming from the rebab music of Rumi to the classic English and French bands of troubadours."

Fellow musician Mickey Zekley wrote about Thomas' early days:

I had been playing folk music on the guitar for a few years but my knowledge was still limited. Bob opened my eyes! In his Catacombs music instruments shop in Pasadena were all manner of antique flutes, strange stringed instruments, gorgeous old bagpipes, unusual ethnic drums, and much more. Bob had taken on the project of researching and restoring all of these and—even more amazing—learning to play them all in their traditional style. Bob would take an ancient set of bagpipes or a hundred-year-old lute out to the Renaissance Faire, dress up in Elizabethan costume and charm everyone.

Thomas passed away in 1993, an unusual pioneer whose career merged graphic artworks with music, renaissance with psychedelic.

The Golden Toad band, featuring Bob Thomas (center) on bagpipes. Grant Street Art Fair, San Francisco, 1969. *Photographer unknown, courtesy The Institute for Traditional Studies*

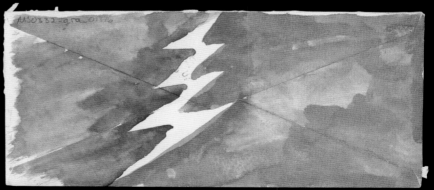

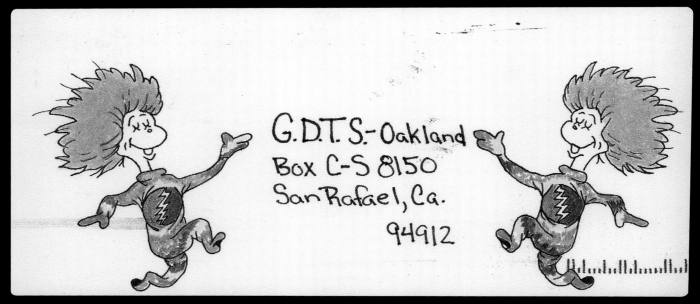

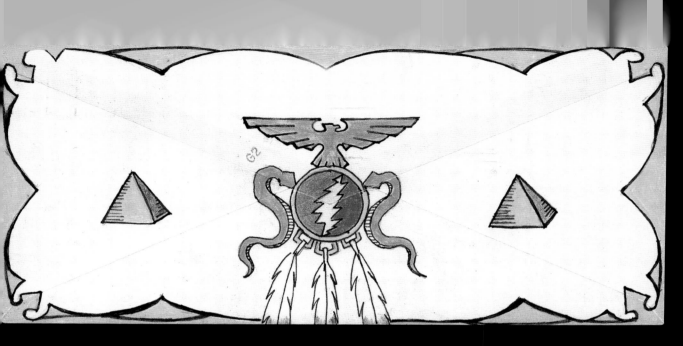

OAKLAND COLISEUM

DEC 31 —
GRATEFUL DEAD
SOLD OUT!

SAN LUIS OBISPO CA 934 2A
PM
22 OCT
1990

ALWAYS
ZIP CODE

USA 25
Yosemite

GRATEFUL DEAD TICKET SALES - NEW YEARS EVE

BOX C-S 8150

SAN RAFAEL, CA 94912

2 TICKETS FOR NEW YEARS EVE PLEASE!

GRATEFUL DEAD Ticket Sales - New Year's '8
P.O. Box C-S8150   1 Ticket
San Rafael, CA.
94912

Grateful Dead
Ticket Sales
Spring Tour Part 2   Knickerbocker Arena
Box C-S 8190
San Rafael,   California
94912

Grateful Dead Ticket Sales - Shoreline
P.O. Box CS-8190
San Rafael, CA 94912

2 ea. 6/18, 6/19
4 ea - 6/21 or anything

THE GREEK THEATRE '88
ADMIT
(2)
TWO
EACH
JULY
15, 16
& 17.

IF THE THUNDER
DON'T GET YOU

THEN THE
LIGHTNING WILL

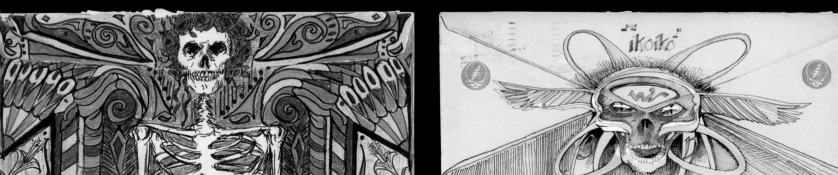

GRATEFUL DEAD
TICKET SALES-
HJK
BOX C-S 8150
SAN RAFAEL
CALIF. 94912

FEB. 5,6,7 - 1 TICKET EACH NIGHT

ikoiko

GRATEFUL DEAD Ticket Sales - Coliseum
Box C-58190
San Rafael, CA.
94912

SEPT 12 & 13
$11 PER NIGHT

New Years

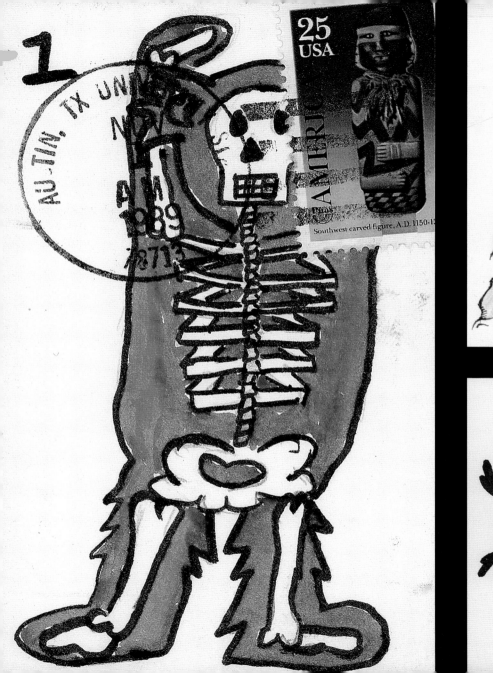

25
USA

AMERICA
Southwest carved figure, A.D. 1150-1...

...87
New England Nep...

Brother Esau
Box C-S 8190
San Rafael • CA.
94912

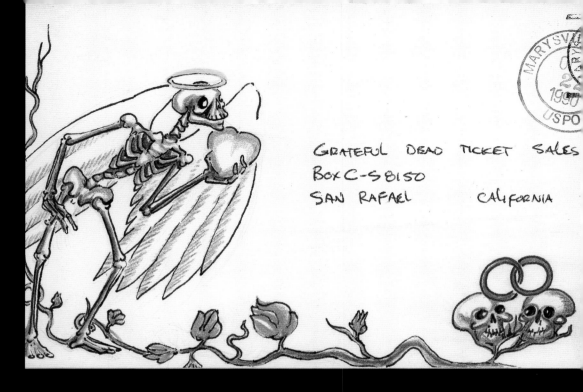

MARYSVILLE
1990
USPO

GRATEFUL DEAD TICKET SALES
BOX C-S 8150
SAN RAFAEL   CALIFORNIA

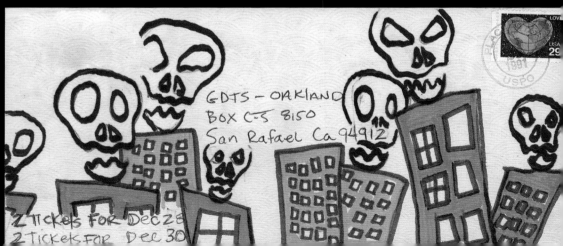

1991
USPO

GDTS - OAKLAND
BOX C-S 8150
San Rafael Ca 94912

2 Tickets For Dec 28
2 Tickets For Dec 30

GRATEFUL DEAD
TICKET SALES
New Year's Eve
BOX C-S8190
SAN RAFAEL, CA 94912

2 TICKETS

Grateful Dead Ticket Sales · New Year's Eve
(2 Tickets)

Box C-S 8190
San Rafael,
California
U.S.A 94912

GRATEFUL DEAD TICKET SALES · NEW YEARS EVE
P.O. BOX C-S8190
SAN RAFAEL, CA 94912

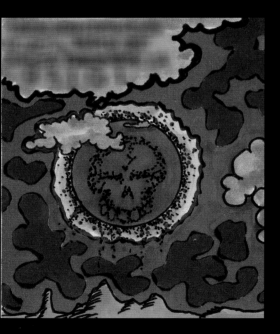

GRATEFUL

December 31st - 2 Tickets

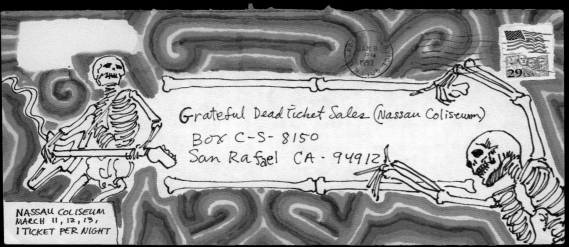

Dead Head Characters

Come and Join the Party Every Day

It is not a cliché to say that Dead Heads come in all different sizes and shapes and with different beliefs. What always fascinated Jerry Garcia was that each Dead Head created his own character and became a player while traveling with the Grateful Dead circus.

This chapter's art proves that conclusively.

Each Dead Head stood out within the group by virtue of circumstance. For example, there are hundreds of stories about a single Head meeting another boy or girl in a crowd of ten thousand, and then meeting that person's friends, and then getting on a bus and afterward traveling on with them. There are just as many stories about arriving at the concert in a van or bus, already surrounded by friends. As united the Dead Heads were in their love for the band, each had a different story about how he or she got there.

Even though each fan felt the love, *how* they felt it was expressed in their own inimitable way. At every Grateful Dead concert there were rows and rows of dancers, but each person went about creating his or her dance in singular fashion.

And every Dead Head had a different opinion about each night. It was good, it was bad, the band was "on" or they were "off" (except for "Dark Star" where they touched the edge of outer space . . . remember?). No opinion was right or

wrong, and all the perceptions were different and yet completely valid in their differences. No one ever saw it the same way—although the Dead Heads (and the band) were united in their opinion when a show was exceptional, when the "fifth man" joined the band so abruptly, so unexpectedly, everyone flying on the same plane, each person personally piloting that plane.

As with classical music, when each person in the house is thinking, "This must be the most wonderful music ever, and no one knows it except for me," something very special happens at Dead concerts. What takes place is a form of group-think on an individual basis. That is the essence of the Grateful Dead experience, and why everyone in a united audience still is his own self-portrait.

You can be straight, you can be high. You can be a complete novice, having attended only one or two concerts, or you could have followed the band over an entire tour. What mattered was you were there. You arrived. You made it. What you *made of it* was entirely your own, hence the diverse portraits in this chapter, all freely submitted without any coaching, without responding to any set rules, without knowing what anybody else might ever say about it. Bob Weir sang, "We are on our own." In "Ripple" Jerry Garcia sang:

> There is a road, no simple highway
> Between the dawn and the dark of night
> And if you go no one may follow
> That path is for your steps alone.

Songs like "Ripple" are uniting visions. But there's a difference between, say, organized religion and the Grateful Dead. There is no dogma at Grateful Dead concerts, other than awareness that particular tunes are being played in a particular order. There is no one at the pulpit telling you what to make of it, what parts to take hold of and believe

OPPOSITE: Every illustration in this chapter is a self-portrait of some kind. Despite some stereotypes, Dead Heads truly are individuals.

This 2008 poster for Phil Lesh and Friends at San Francisco's Warfield Theater was designed by Dennis Larkins and art-directed by Arlene Owseichik as one in a six-part poster series for a run of shows. All six posters depicted dancing, clothed skeletons. © 2008 Bill Graham Presents. Used by permission

in. There is no road map, no *one way*. It's simply, believe it if you feel it.

All this can be said for celebrity Dead Heads as well, of which there are hundreds. Bill Walton, who wrote this book's compelling foreword, may be a storied NBA champion, but he dances his own dance just like anyone out there, a dance to whatever drummer he's hearing.

A Grateful Dead concert could—and did—have Nancy Pelosi (the first woman Speaker of the House) and Ann Coulter (commentator from the far right) in attendance, each a million miles apart in terms of political beliefs but nevertheless joined at the hip because of their affection for the Dead. Both have agreed, independently, and in print, that the scene was "irresistible."

Celebrity affection could be as true-blue as that of the most unknown Dead Head, and vice-versa.

Broadcast journalist and anchorman Walter Cronkite was a self-professed Dead Head, even as he was celebrated as "the most trusted man in America." The president of CBS News and Sports, Sean McManus, said at Cronkite's funeral, "Walter loved music, he loved the Grateful Dead. The Dead adopted him, and he adopted them. He was totally their fan."

Cronkite once saw an entire Grateful Dead show at Madison Square Garden from the soundboard. He later said it was one of his fondest moments. In a 2004 interview with *Details* magazine, Cronkite enthused, "Mickey Hart is a good friend of mine," as he showed off a giant gong in his office. "Mickey's a real expert on percussion instruments around the world. And he gave me that lovely thing. You can play a full song on it, it's so beautifully tuned. It's quite remarkable. It's from Tibet."

Hart performed at Cronkite's funeral and afterward said, "He told me straight out, 'I love your music.' He was an honest, truthful guy that used his power while he was here on Earth well. He was for the good. And he was a fan of the Grateful Dead. You know, during the Madison Square Garden show, he came backstage at halftime and I introduced him to Jerry. Walter said, 'I was thinking of a thousand reasons to leave early, but I can't think of one now.' He stayed until the last note was played."

President Barack Obama thanked members of the band in the Oval Office, as did Bill Clinton, but they are not really Dead Heads—at least not with quite the same fervor as former Vice President Al Gore (and even more so his wife Tipper); Senators Patrick Leahy, Al Franken, Barbara Boxer, and Harry Reid (who has a Grateful Dead poster in his bathroom on the Hill); former Massachusetts Governor William Weld; and, of course, Representative Pelosi.

Tony Blair, England's former prime minister, played in a band called Ugly Rumours while a student at Oxford University. (The band's name was a take on the cover art to *Grateful Dead from the Mars Hotel*.) Blair's successor, Gordon Brown, appointed Alex Allan to head Britain's Joint Intelligence Committee. Allan's favorite group had long been the Dead. "I was there in the mud at Bickershaw in 1972," he said. "I was so knocked out I've been a Dead Head ever since."

Pete Carroll, the hugely successful football coach at University of Southern California (now coach of the Seattle Seahawks) is a longtime Dead Head, as is Phil Jackson, the cerebral head coach of the Los Angeles Lakers. Jim Irsay, owner of the Indianapolis Colts, is a fascinating Dead Head. He purchased Jerry Garcia's "Tiger" guitar at auction and is rumored to bring guitars on Colts road trips and play until three in the morning.

Philosopher Joseph Campbell, Fox News commentator Tucker Carlson (who conducted an in-depth interview with Phil Lesh), and actor Whoopi Goldberg have all been major fans. For them, too, it's all about recognizing art at a truly high level, parallel to whatever they've created themselves, but none are any more knowledgeable about Grateful Dead arcanum than the average Dead Head.

Equally fascinating are the range of musicians who've expressed admiration for the Dead's songwriting and musicianship, and in their own way would be called Dead Heads. Obviously that list includes musicians who played with the Dead for lengthy periods or on special occasions—Merl Saunders, Bruce Hornsby, Warren Haynes, David Crosby, John Cipollina, Joan Baez, and others. More head-turning are those from other genres who listened to the Dead and even reinterpreted some of the band's songs—Henry Rollins, Greg Ginn (from Black Flag), Elvis Costello, Frank Marino (of Mahogany Rush), Perry Farrell (Jane's Addiction). Others briefly became Dead Heads of a sort (the Dead having backed them in concert or asked them to jam or to open)—Bob Dylan, Hamza el-Din, John Belushi and Dan Aykroyd of the Blues Brothers, and jazz greats Branford Marsalis and Ornette Coleman.

Of course, bands like Phish, the String Cheese Incident, Dark Star Orchestra, and Umphrey's McGee owe much to the Dead for establishing a jam-band philosophy and belong to their own category of friends within the extended Dead Head family.

What the Dead Heads recognized in creating these decorated envelopes with their own portraits is that everybody is his own star, celebrity or regular Joe. Everyone stands out in the land of the Grateful Dead.

GEN. ADM.
OR
ANYTHING

GRATEFUL DEAD TICKET SALES
P.O. BOX C-S 8150
San RAFAEL, CA.
94912

GREENSBORO
N.C.
30TH
31ST

BZZT

BZZT

BZZT

25 USA

Grateful Dead ticket Sales - The Omni
Box C-F 8150
San Raphael, Ca. 94912

1992

The Omni
03-01-92 - one (1) ticket
03-02-92 - one (1) ticket
03-03-92 - one (1) ticket

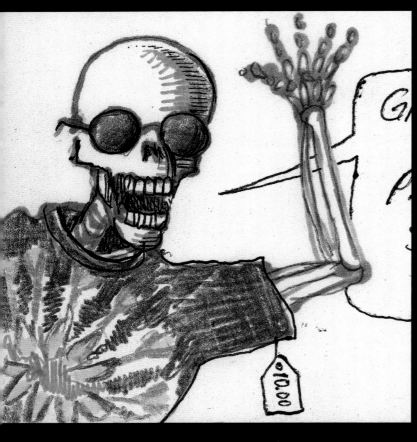

GRATEFUL DEAD
TICKET SALES

FROST

NARD CA 930 B2
PM
APR '87

USA 22

P.O. BOX
C-S 8190
SAN RAFAEL, CA
94912

Bart Kline
2441 Roanoke Dr.
Boise, ID
83712

BOISE
OCT 22 1990

Marianne Moore
25 USA
American Poet 1889-1972

GRATEFUL DEAD ticket sales - OAKLAND
P.O. BOX C-S8190
SAN RAFAEL CA
94912

GRATEFUL DEAD
TICKET SALES - SPECTRUM
BOX C-S 8190
SAN RAFAEL, CA
94912

Domestic USA

9-9-88
4 TICKETS

SAN JOSE CA 951
PM
NOV
1989

S EVE

Begin an Adventure of
Giant Proportion!
Collect Stamps!

LOVE

1965-1990

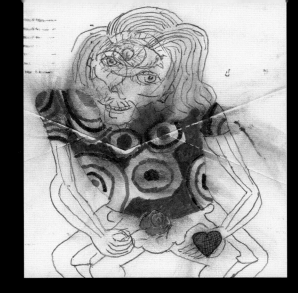

LOVE
USA
1995

GDTS · Knickerbocker Arena
Box CS 8190
San Rafael Ca.
1 94912

nickerbocker 2 for June 21
2 for June 22

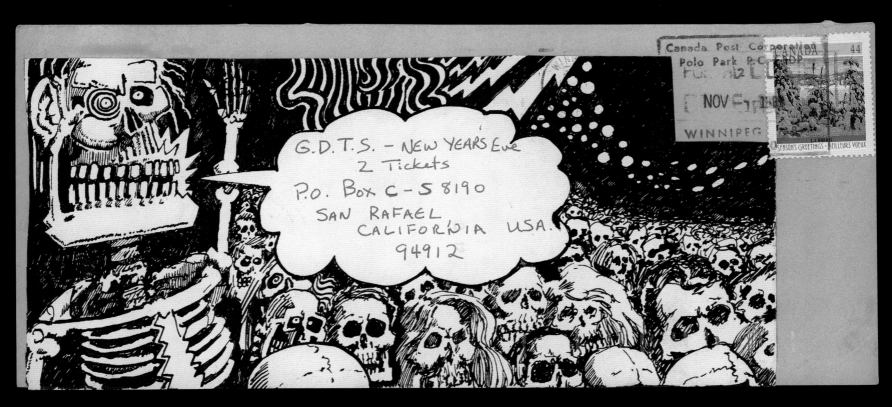

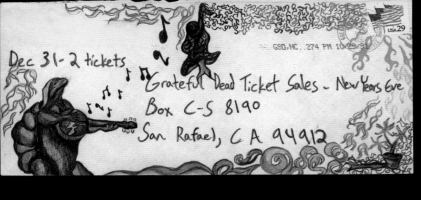

Dec 31 - 2 tickets

Grateful Dead Ticket Sales - New Years Eve
Box C-S 8190
San Rafael, CA 94912

GREET THE MORNING AIR WITH SONG

GRATEFUL DEAD
TICKET SALES - IRVINE
BOX C-S 8150
SAN RAFAEL, CA 94912

GRATEFUL DEAD
TICKET SALES - LANDOVER
Box C-S 8150
San Raphael, Calf. 94912

Mar. 8 - 1 ticket
Mar. 9 - 1 ticket

HAPPY NEW YEAR!

POP

NEW YEARS!

HEY NOW!!

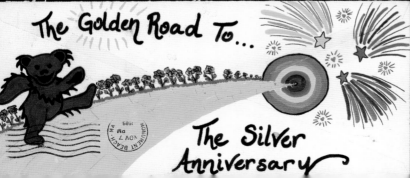

The Golden Road To...

The Silver Anniversary

GRATE

SA

~ALYSA~

2- TICKETS   DEC 31, 19

2 tickets
new years eve

P.O. Box

Grateful Dead Ticket Sales Shoreline
Box C-S 8150
San Rafael, CA
94912

One ticket for each show

← CORK

Happy New Years

December 31st - 2 tickets

GRATEFUL DEAD TICKET
SALES-CHINESE
BOX C-S 8150
SAN RAFAEL, CA.
94912

G.D.T.S. (LAS VEGAS)
BOX CS-8190
SAN RAFAEL, CA.
94912
SAT. 5/15
SUN. 5/16

Grateful Dead
Ticket Sales Shoreline
Box C-S ~ 8150 San Rafael, Ca, 94912

Grateful Dead
· TICKET SALES ·
SPRING TOUR PART II: MIAMI
P.O. BOX C-S 8150
SAN RAFAEL, CA. 94912
2 TKTS. 4/6 · 2 TKTS 4/7

IKO IKO
DA SN !!!

GRATEFUL DEAD TICKET SALES
-THE GREEK-
BOX C-S 8150
SAN RAFAEL, CA 94912

TWO (2) TICKETS FOR SATURDAY 7-16

Grateful Dead Ticket Sales - R.F.K.
P.O. Box C-S 8190
San Rafael, CA 94912

Please send 8
June 24, 25
1 ticket each, general admission

ALWAYS
USE ZIP CODE

Grateful Dead ticket Sales
P.O. BOX ——→ C-S 8190
San Raphael, ca. 94912

(madison Sq. Garden - 2 tix each night)

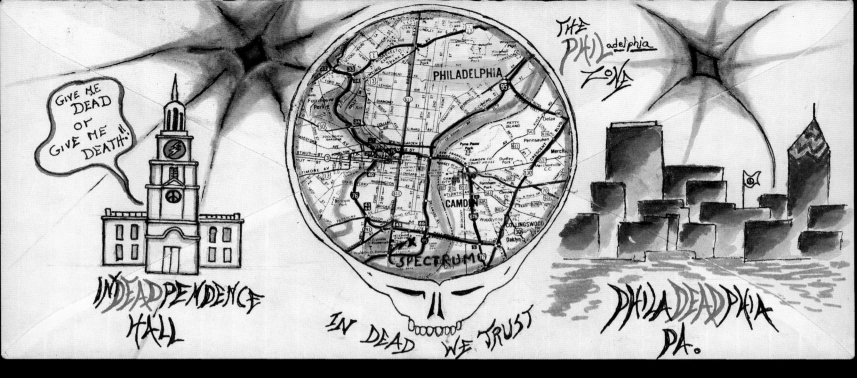

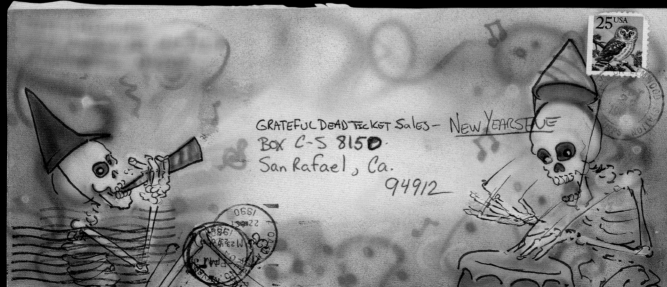

Grateful Dead Ticket Sales-Schlyer Field-July 8
6 Tickets
Box C-S 8190
SAN RAFAEL, CA 94912

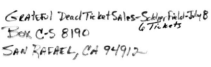

SARATOGA →

Grateful Dead Ticket Sales - Saratoga
BOX C-S 8190
San Rafael, CA. 94912

ALLAN THOMPSON © '88

2 NEW YEARS EVE TICKETS.

2 tickets to
New Year's please
(or refund)

GRATEFUL
BOX C-S
SAN RAF

2 FOR APRIL 22ND
3 FOR " 23RD
2 FOR " 24TH OR ANYTHING

Grateful Dead Ticket Sales - New Year's Eve
Box C-S 8150
San Rafael, California
94912

When we make it to the Promised Land!

GRATEFUL DEAD TICKET SALES - OAKLAND
Box C-S 8150
SAN RAFAEL, CALIFORNIA 94912

GRATEFUL DEAD TICKET SALES: AUBURN HILLS
Box C-S 8150   3/23: 2 TICKETS
San Rafael, CA 94912   3/24: 2 TICKETS

'Shrooms, Tie Dye & Flying Eyeballs

Every Once in a While You Get Shown the Light

No book about the Grateful Dead experience could avoid the topic of psychedelics.

A plurality of Dead Heads would say that in all of rock 'n' roll (with the possible exception of Pink Floyd) Grateful Dead concerts are those best suited for such higher adventures in psychic exploration. The Grateful Dead in particular evolved a concert format that provided an up-and-down continuum of music-making, confusing the fans for long periods (in, say, second-set "Space") and then resolving all doubts and fears by peaking spectacularly in transformative songs like "Morning Dew," "Sugar Magnolia," or "Not Fade Away." This concert progression mirrored that of the psychedelic drug-aided journey, the "trip." Dead Head–decorated envelopes rarely portrayed the scientific molecular geometry for hallucinogens, but an enormous number were adorned with magic mushrooms, which can be rendered in every imaginable shape, size, and color.

Two bands, actually, shared an abiding interest in mushrooms, the other being the Allman Brothers Band. Much of the iconography rendered on countless Allman Brothers T-shirts and concert posters includes psychedelic mushrooms. The Dead never embraced the mushroom as an official graphic but were delighted to see that their fan base had a field day with them and understood that 'shrooms illuminated the far corners of the mind, sharpened the acuity of the senses, and were the root cause for many a great group good time (most often at Grateful Dead concerts).

Dead Heads should know, however, they were not the first to turn on with mushrooms. The oldest graphics showing mushrooms are in the Sahara Desert, produced 7,000 to 9,000 years ago. These rock paintings were the works of pre-Neolithic gatherers. Such ancient artworks, as well as depictions of god-like figures covered in mushrooms, led experts to believe in the existence of many ancient mushroom cults.

Scholars have also discovered ancient interest in these hallucinogens in Algeria, Egypt, Chad, India, Greece, and to the south in Mesoamerica, Mexico, and in particular the Dominican Republic. In California the history of the Chumash and Yokut Native Americans includes their partaking in mescal derivatives and peyote as part of their religious observances. Approximately 190 species of psilocybin mushrooms are spread around the world, so it seems likely other cultures "turned on" as well.

The Dead Heads, representing a modern tribe of seekers, not surprisingly fit the historical profile of a human group discovering a botanical means to explore releases from normal boundaries. Today this is expressed with the phrase "achieving a higher state of consciousness" or, more simply, "getting high." Jerry Garcia was asked by Charles Reich and Jann Wenner in their book *Garcia: A Signpost to New Space* (1972) why it was so important to get high. Garcia responded:

> To get really high, like what we did at the Acid Tests, is to forget yourself. And to forget yourself is to see everything else. And to see everything else is to become an understanding

OPPOSITE: With roots in American hot rod culture (and ancient Egypt) the flying eyeball has found its way onto many an envelope whose sender wanted to impress his or her hipness on the Dead's ticket office.

molecule in evolution, a conscious tool of the universe. And I think every human being should be a conscious tool of the universe.

The Acid Tests were our first exposure to formlessness. Formlessness and chaos lead to new forms, new order, closer to, probably, what the real order is. So I think of the Grateful Dead as being a crossroads or a pointer sign—maybe a signpost to New Space—and what we're pointing to is that there's a lot of universe still available for exploration.

Tie-dye has long been a part of the Grateful Dead experience, too. One of the greatest tie-dye artists in America, Courtenay Pollock, a master of the mandala, created tie-dyed fabric covers used for the Dead's onstage speakers from 1969 to 1972. His work really took hold in 1970 when he was in residence at Bob Weir's Rucka Rucka Ranch in Marin County and Weir and fellow band mate Bill Kreutzmann began wearing tie-dyed T-shirts on stage.

Ten years later, Bill Graham Presents invited Pollock to create an entire tie-dyed stage backdrop for the band's Berkeley Greek Theater run, and he reprised it with a whole new set of sixteen matching tie-dyed panels the following year in 1983.

"The geometric Mandala is the circle of life, the 'wheel' of world within worlds," Pollack writes on his website. "It's an ancient art form, used in Buddhism, Hinduism, and in Japanese, Malay, Balinese, and Native American cultures. In the context of the Grateful Dead specifically, tie-dye represents a colorful circle of family and friends."

The tie-dyed Grateful Dead T-shirt is an American icon all its own, although it was not the costume of the original Haight-Ashbury hippies. Artists like Mikio, Michael Everett, Ralph Mannis, and Phil Brown, and companies like Charlotte's Dye Works, Liquid Blue, and Not Fade Away popularized incandescent colors on wearables beginning in the late 1970s, pulling from the vibrancy of the psychedelic rock poster.

LEFT: The Grateful Dead shared an abiding interest in mushrooms with the Allman Brothers Band. Much of the iconography rendered on countless Allmans T-shirts and concert posters includes psychedelic mushrooms. ©2010 ABB Merchandising Co., Inc.

RIGHT: The flying eyeball had deep roots in hot rod culture. So did Stanley Mouse. He and Alton Kelley rendered their own version for their Monster Company studio (aka Monster Corporation of America).

Every hand-dyed garment is unique. Dead Head–decorated envelopes emulated that, wowing the ticket office with individualized patterns created with ink or colored pencil rather than dye.

The flying eyeball, in its own innumerable renditions, was also included on many decorated envelopes to impress the ticket office with the sender's hipness. As frequently as it appeared, it was not an official Grateful Dead mark.

Kenneth Howard, a.k.a. Von Dutch, was a genius automobile pinstriper who is said to have drawn his first flying eyeball in 1948. Not long after, other well-known lowbrow and hot rod "kustom culture" artists created their own versions. Prominent among them were Ed "Big Daddy" Roth, who went from the flying eyeball to his Rat Fink character, and Dean Jeffries.

According to Von Dutch, the flying eyeball actually originated with the Macedonian and Egyptian cultures about 5,000 years ago. Dutch believed in reincarnation, and he believed the eyeball was tied to such reappearance. Whatever it actually stood for, it became an icon of the 1950s and '60s hot rod crowd and, in the new millennium, the genesis of a hip clothing line.

Rick Griffin, master cartoonist for the So-Cal surf scene, moved to San Francisco in 1967 to join what poster artist Stanley Mouse called a "really juicy scene." For a February 1968 poster promoting a Jimi Hendrix concert at Bill Graham's Fillmore Auditorium, Griffin used his own version of the flying eyeball. It became a classic, known worldwide (although its genesis is often incorrectly attributed to Griffin). Griffin added serpent-like tentacles to the winged, bloodshot, all-seeing eye. Subsequently, he included surfing eyeballs on one of his two signature Grateful Dead pieces, the "Hawaiian Aoxomoxoa" poster, and on many other surf-themed artworks.

Fellow artists Stanley Mouse, who had roots in the hot rod culture, and studio partner Alton Kelley rendered their own version for their just-opened Monster Company in 1971, adding even more three-dimensional tentacles, as did Santa Cruz's Jim Phillips in his surf and skateboard artworks.

All of these versions—Von Dutch to Phillips—were noticed by the Dead Heads. Not surprisingly, then, the eyeballs depicted on ticket-request envelopes were shown to be playing onstage at Grateful Dead concerts, surfing monster waves at beaches around the country, and generally insinuating themselves into a hundred different, yes, "juicy" scenes.

TO:
GRATEFUL DEAD
TICKET SALES
S.F. CIVIC AUD.
WHARF RAT
P.O. BOX C-S 8150
SAN RAFAEL
CALIFORNIA
94912

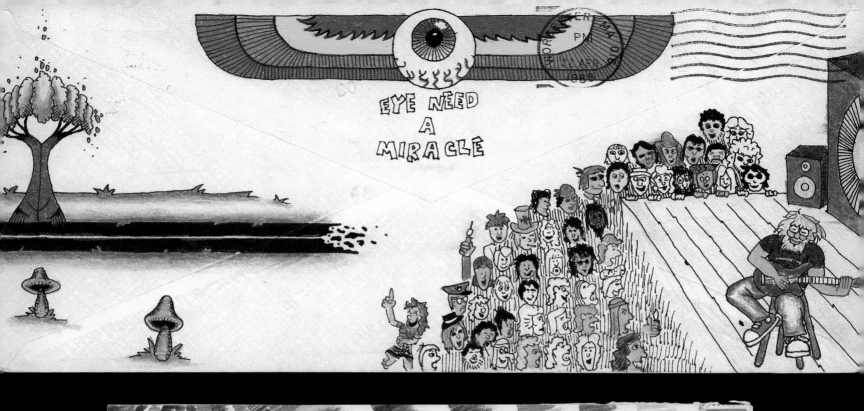

EYE NEED A MIRACLE

GDTS — New Years Eve
P.O. Box C-S 8190
San Rafael, CA 94912

2 Tickets NEW Years Eve

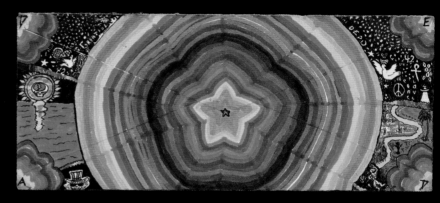

RIGHT MIDDLE: Artist: Seth Worden

USA 25

Grateful Dead Ticket Sales - Philly
Box C-S 8150
San Rafael, CA 94912

2 TICKETS   10-18-89
2 TICKETS   10-19-89
2 TICKETS   10-20-89

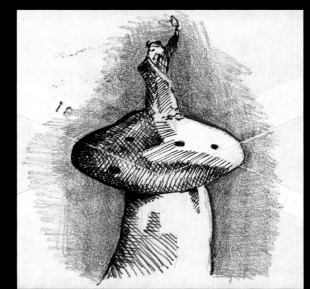

SAN FRAN...PM
29 OCT
1991

GDTS-Oakland
Box C-S 8150
San Rafael, CA
94912

DEC. 27, 28, 30
1 ticket EACH Nite
OR ANYTHING, PLEASE.

GRATEFUL DEAD
BOX C-S 8150
San Rafael, Ca.
94912

TICKET SALES-
SPECTRUM
PHILLY
PENNSYLVANIA

3/16 - 2 TICKETS
3/18 - 3 TICKETS

LANCA
JAN 15
1992
USA
29

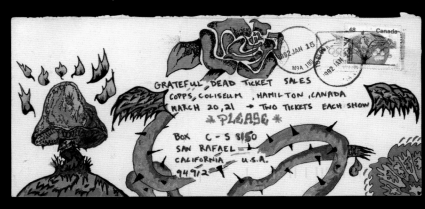

GRATEFUL DEAD TICKET SALES
COPPS COLISEUM, HAMILTON, CANADA
MARCH 20, 21 → TWO TICKETS EACH SHOW
* PLEASE *
BOX C-S 8150
SAN RAFAEL
CALIFORNIA U.S.A.
94912

1992 JAN 15
M9A 190

48 Canada

137

138

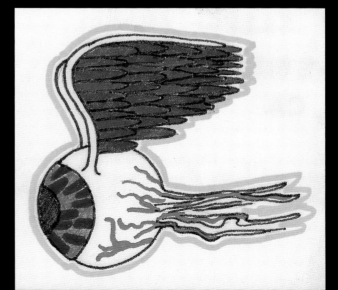

CHAPTER 12

The Band Members

I'm Just Playing in the Band

Hers was *the one*. It was published in the *Grateful Dead: The Official Book of the Dead Heads*, and still has instant recognition value. That would be Barbara Carr's "Captain Trips" portrait of Jerry Garcia spotted by Eileen Law and Nadine Kaplan on an incoming envelope in the early 1970s. It was so magnificent that it was immediately pinned to the first-floor bulletin board inside the kitchen at the Dead's 5th and Lincoln headquarters in San Rafael. Everybody admired it. Garcia himself loved it.

How could you not?

It was done freehand. It wasn't re-illustrated from a photograph. It had sparkles in the ink. The proportions were pleasing, and Garcia's alter ego, Captain Trips, had a spacey-stern look about him that was thoroughly engaging.

This was not a ticket-request envelope, rather a simple letter of thanks, but the illustration would stand the test of time and become the standard by which all other decorated envelopes would be judged. This was caricature at its finest, Dead Head style.

During the 1970s and early 1980s many Dead Head letters contained portraits of Garcia and sometimes other band members. Some were redrawings of famous photos, like those Stanley Mouse took for the front and back cover

of *Workingman's Dead* (1970), or Bob Seidemann's 5th and Lincoln parking lot portrait that graced the inside of "Skull & Roses" (1971).

Quite a number of the portraits were twisted visions, not always flattering. Heartfelt no doubt, but also weird and uncomfortable to look at in some cases. Eileen saved all of these but did not necessarily post them in the kitchen. She had long ago accepted that one person's vision was no less valid than another's, but maybe some were best just tucked away.

There was no censorship in Dead Head arts and letters. People sent in what they sent in. But, when decorated ticket-request envelopes became a key element in the Dead's new business enterprise, there was a new level of judgment, and competition, involved.

Although homage to the band members was not nearly as popular a subject as the Stealie, lightning bolt, terrapin, dancing bears, or even the flying eyeball, it was there all the same, every hundred envelopes or so, now readily apparent in the chronologically arranged file boxes at the Grateful Dead Archive at University of California, Santa Cruz. Once again, not all the art portraying the band members was flattering, although there was equality in its utilitarian purpose: good art or bad art, every envelope contained a money order.

The best portraits were intuitive caricatures. Those caught everyone's eye at Grateful Dead Ticket Sales. But those that were obvious re-illustrations of photos, or which simply used glued-on photos, were generally not thought of so highly. They were not singularly interpretive, and the human spirit did not respond to them very readily. So, for the relatively brief period when the "best" decorated envelopes got the first-round-

---

OPPOSITE: Band member portraits were not nearly as popular as the Stealie, skull, bear, or other band icons, but they showed up on fan-decorated envelopes just the same—on about every one hundred envelopes or so, if the files at UCSC are any indication.

of-ticket-pulls attention, the "best" portraits were among those envelopes grabbed. But soon enough, given the ever-increasing volume of incoming envelopes, the choice pretty much became a grab bag. Anyone at GDTS could have thrown darts at a wall of portrait-decorated envelopes—with skilled and amateurish illustrations in equal measure—and made the same random choice of who would receive tickets.

Certainly there was a wide range of skill involved in creating Grateful Dead band member caricature. Some of it was very, very good, witty, and funny. Others with their portraits, honestly speaking, were fairly pathetic. But it all came from the same place: the heart (or at least the common desire to score tickets).

Caricature has long played a role in the graphic portrayal of the San Francisco music scene. You only have to remember Robert Crumb's illustrations for Big Brother and the Holding Company's *Cheap Thrills* (1968) to see a master portraitist-cartoonist at work. Rick Griffin was a renowned cartoonist in the Southern California surf scene, with a legendary strip in *Surfer* magazine featuring the character

Murphy, before he moved north to San Francisco in 1967 and began creating psychedelic posters and major artworks for the Dead. Another member of the legendary "Big Five" San Francisco poster artists was Victor Moscoso, who along with Crumb set new standards for twisted caricature in *Zap Comix*. Later, he illustrated several Jerry Garcia solo albums.

Other caricaturists whose work influenced that of the Dead Heads' included Ralph Steadman (Hunter S. Thompson's *Fear and Loathing in Las Vegas*, 1971) and Gerald Scarfe (Pink Floyd's *The Wall*, 1979).

Not that it would have directly affected the head-space of most Dead Heads particularly, but the history of biting, scathing, *pointed* caricature begins with people like George Cruikshank (1792–1878), Honoré Daumier (1808–1879), Thomas Nast (1840–1902), Sir Max Beerbohm (1872–1956), and political cartoonists like Herblock (who fired away for decades at the *Washington Post*).

Dead Heads certainly would have seen the more contemporary Al Hirschfeld (1903–2003), who published magnificent caricatures both of

the Grateful Dead and Jerry Garcia. Garcia, a fine artist himself and a great collector of comics (and comix), was influenced by, among others, caricaturist Mort Drucker (born 1929), who illustrated for *MAD* magazine.

Among the Dead Head illustrators, Barry Haden's artworks stand out (see Chapter 13), and his own self-portraits and pen-and-ink portraits of Garcia are proof that caricature is alive and well in the hands of a highly capable, intuitive artist.

It comes as no surprise that Garcia inspired the greatest number of portraits, followed by Pigpen. Many times Garcia and Weir were successfully linked (see Chapter 14) and occasionally the drummers were the focus of an artist's attention. Phil Lesh was several times portrayed as a NASA scientist. Of the keyboardists, blondie Brent Mydland was rendered with the most affection.

Garcia himself appreciated the good wishes but not all the attention. Yet, he could not escape the fact that all eyes were on him. While he would not have encouraged the up-close-and-personal approach, over the transom it came nonetheless. Year after year after year.

So we have to be grateful for Barbara Carr's inspirational vision. Yes, it was Captain Trips (a title Garcia rarely acknowledged), but her portrait was handled in such a way that you could just *feel* the love.

Stanley Mouse, Alton Kelley, Rick Griffin, Victor Moscoso . . . meet Barbara. Now that's an accomplishment.

Barbara Carr's "Captain Trips" portrait of Jerry Garcia is so magnificent that it was immediately pinned to the first-floor bulletin board inside the kitchen at the Dead's 5th and Lincoln headquarters in San Rafael. Everybody admired it, including Garcia.

Keep on TRUCKIN!

CHAPTER 13

The Second Set

Sometimes the Light's All Shining on Me

This is the "second set" chapter of *Dead Letters*, the place where things get real wiggy, illustratively speaking. Of course, the second set is where the Dead themselves got real wiggy, where on a great night they took off for the four corners, taking the entire audience on a wild improvisational ride.

Beginning in 1971, thousands of Dead Head letters and artworks now in the UCSC Grateful Dead Archive attest to what took place in the second set. Beginning in 1983, so did the decorated envelopes.

This chapter's selected envelopes are marvelous vignettes, intuitively accomplished attempts by Dead Heads to graphically interpret the Grateful Dead second set gestalt. So, unlike the envelopes in the other chapters, these are nonspecific to songs, lyrics, or concerts. These simply are visions, just like the real thing.

This is where improvisational music, on-the-precipice graphics, and nearly off-the-road prose have their overlap.

In Grateful Dead arts and letters, there are at least three notable prose accounts of full-blown second sets. The first is Michael Lydon's August 23, 1969, *Rolling Stone* article (later included in his 1971 classic *Rock Folk*). This writing concerned the Dead's May 30, 1969, appearance at the obscure Springer's Inn

in Gresham, Oregon, a suburb of Portland, where the band only played three times (the other two times in 1970). Lydon's piece concludes with a just-on-the-edge-of-out-of-control rendition of an epic hour-long "Dark Star" into "Cosmic Charlie" into "St. Stephen" into "The Eleven" into "Turn on Your Lovelight."

Ah, you had to be there. Actually, we know one person besides Lydon who was.

"I was one of the first to get to the parking lot at Springer's for the May show," blogged Loren E. in November 2010. "We (Nancy, Greg, and myself) got there early because the parking lot was so small. Loren E. continues:

> We watched what had to be one of the Dead's all-time shows. We danced till it hurt and danced still more. It was epic! It was beyond epic!
>
> Since we were one of the first vehicles in, we'd be one of the last to leave. We were standing around for a long time just trying to catch our breath, take stock of what had just happened. Finally I got in and started to back out of our parking spot. Suddenly the whole band, with their girlfriends, came walking by.
>
> I jokingly said as I was leaning out the window, "Hey Jer, you need a lift?" And to my utter shock he answered in that high-pitched voice of his, "Hey man, thanks, we had to park our van about a mile up the road."
>
> That night I happened to be driving my 1940 Chevy Sedan Delivery, with its really big running boards along the side. Within seconds the entire band jumped on and all the girls jumped in, and we made it very slowly through the crowd out to their van. What a scene!
>
> As everyone was piling off, Pigpen pointed out that, with all the added weight from everyone, my fenders probably had destroyed

OPPOSITE: Dead Heads often attempted to interpret the band's second-set gestalt—that segment of Dead shows where the band got real wiggy.

my rear tires—nice new ones too. Of course I told him "That's fine!" because I had just had the whole band in my '40 Chev and besides the show I'd have that memory with me for the rest of my life.

Enduring recollection is also what sets apart the second example, Ed McClanahan's March 1972 essay in *Playboy* entitled "Grateful Dead I Have Known," later included in *My Vita, If You Will* (1998). McClanahan, a close friend of Ken Kesey, was a fine interviewer but an even finer observer. His account of how Pigpen brought an entire concert to its knees remains a stunning work of art. The piece simply builds and builds and builds until the reader's mind is left disheveled and the venue has exploded in one last spasm of joy . . . precisely what the Dead had in mind that night for the audience.

Some say the third of the three most notable second set renditions is this author's own "Second Set Notes" that appeared in *Grateful Dead: The Official Book of the Dead Heads.* This prose poem

was egged on by the skillful editing of the Dead's de facto head of publishing, Alan Trist. This poetry mimicked thousands of tapers' stream-of-consciousness between-and-during-songs jottings, and many Dead Heads to this day believe it was a capture of an actual, specific everything-you-wished-for concert.

Maybe it was, maybe it wasn't. I ain't tellin'.

Three artists also are highlighted here: Damian Strahl, Dan Nettell, and Barry Haden. Their work blew away the good people at Grateful Dead Ticket Sales repeatedly. Their envelopes stood out among all the millions received.

Damian Strahl was an accomplished painter. He's no longer with us, but Steve Silberman, coauthor of *Skeleton Key*, remembers him as "an awkwardly tall, gentle, exquisitely sarcastic man." Strahl, who made his home in Berkeley, California, was an early visitor to the WELL, the birthplace of the conversation-based online community.

Strahl kept an online journal on the WELL, from which this is excerpted:

Baseball used to be my metaphor for life and then I saw the Dead and realized that there were situations wherein *everybody* wins. I can still sit in the bleachers and spin a deft allegory based on what's happening on the field, but the years of traveling the Dead cultural frontier has given me the gift of discovering that metaphors can jump out at you in any given moment, in any place or situation.

In his journal, Strahl also addressed his own evolving physical situation head on, much as Robert Hunter's protagonist in "Black Peter" did his. Wrote Strahl:

My own father's death was the heaviest burden of mortality I have had to bear. It changed the way I understood life and death like no on else's passing before or since. Lennon and Garcia's passing feel big too because of their huge symbolic and iconographic legacy, but my father is in me to the core and he continues to reveal himself at the oddest moments, in the turn

GRATEFUL DEAD TICKET SALES
P.O BOX C-S 8190
SAN RAFAEL, CA
94912

NEW YEARS EVE

2 TICKETS - Dec. 31st

USA 29
Basketball
Centennial 1991

Melson

GDTS TOO

They Say That When Your Ship Comes In

How much has really changed over the years? Grateful Dead Ticket Sales (GDTS) was a totally self-administered mail-order ticketing operation run by one of the world's top-grossing touring rock bands from 1983 to 1995. Midway through the band's final decade, close to 50 percent of the Dead's income from ticket sales was the result of having assembled a devoted and dedicated crew that created and administered the mail-order system.

The work environment was almost always fun and exciting but involved hard work and long, long hours. The constancy of effort evolved into ironclad procedure and is what sustained the income flow as well as nurtured the corporate development of GDTS and subsequently GDTS TOO (the new ticketing company that was incorporated after the passing of Jerry Garcia in 1995).

In the very beginning, it was learn-on-the go. An airtight dispersal system had to be designed and books had to balance. As the demand for tickets grew, more efficient ways of serving the masses of mail order requests were required.

Co-manager Steven Marcus, among much else, would order the tickets, cleverly designed to frustrate counterfeiters. Supervisor Calico Van Der Mei would oversee and personally sort the incoming mail and determine the ticket requests that could be honored. Co-manager Frankie Accardi-Peri would hire

the full ticketing crews, interact with the halls, and balance the books. Other supervisors handled customer service and postal-service registration (getting the tickets to the Dead Heads safely and on time).

What evolved was sophistication, a long way from the first mail-order fulfillment. "For those first shows, in Billy Grillo's living room on Front Street in San Rafael, we posted a giant seating chart of the Warfield Theater on the wall, and marked off each seat for each concert as it was sold," said Steven. "I remember Eddie Washington, Calico, Michelle Trahan, and me sprawled on the floor filling orders . . . it was a new and fun time, and not particularly sophisticated. It was also very challenging because we hadn't yet invented all the procedures."

While some aspects of the procedures changed over time (phone-bank Hotline messages that once announced the concert tours have been replaced by more efficient Internet announcements), Dead Heads still must honor the postmark dates to be successful with their purchase requests. Many of the basic mail-order tenets that developed within GDTS survived the transition to GDTS TOO.

GDTS mail orders were processed on a first-come, first-served basis by the date an order was postmarked. However, if there were more postmarked orders for the first mail-order date than tickets, GDTS would collect all those ticket orders and employ a random selection process for filling the orders (and that included some element of honoring the decorated envelopes, just as it still does today).

The key for any successful transaction for any Dead Head was to get a ticket request postmarked on the first day of mail order for the desired show. If the mail order date was, say, June 1, then it was almost incumbent on the purchaser to have a postal employee hand postmark the ordering envelope that day.

OPPOSITE: The long, strange trip may have ended with Jerry Garcia's passing in 1995, but ticket requests for the many projects of surviving members continue to flow into GDTS TOO.

As well, all the analog-style instructions involving #10 envelopes, 3x5 index cards, U.S. Postal or American Express money orders, the proper number of U.S. stamps outside, and similarly correctly putting the correct number of stamps on the return envelope inside, were critical. Clarity in communications regarding the number of tickets desired, the name of the concert, and the name and address of the ticket purchaser, were beyond important in order for Grateful Dead mail order to succeed—then or now. Due to the volume and regularity of its business, GDTS mail-order personnel also became part of San Rafael's downtown social community. Also in the community, there was the involvement of dozens of workers at the post office, the bank, and at Grateful Dead Productions and merchandising.

"I remember one afternoon, early on, maybe in 1984, sitting in the office, with several of us gathered in a circle to pre-visualize the impact of four trays of mail [300 to 400 envelopes per tray] that we forecasted would arrive the next morning. We were absolutely *awestruck* when forty trays arrived!" said Frankie.

Within just the first year or two, the band's popularity as processed through mail order had once again exploded. New measures for ticketing and security had to be implemented and the number of people composing each tasked crew increased dramatically. Along with Steven, Frankie, and Calico, other GDTS supervisors became instrumental in delivering tens of thousands of successful transactions during this transition to a much larger fan base. These heroes are Forrest Schofield, Mary Knudsen, Tom Reed, Carol Latvala, and Joanne Wishnoff. Today, Mary continues to serve GDTS TOO.

GDTS supervisor Forrest Schofield moved to California in 1980 to live and work in Mill Valley. Beginning in 1983 he was an employee at the popular Station Café in San Rafael, near the 5th and

Lincoln Grateful Dead headquarters. By the end of 1987 he'd met many GDTS folks through common friends in Berkeley, at Bay Area Dead concerts, and at the restaurant. The café laid him off in January 1988 and immediately he was hired at GDTS, where he was a supervisor until 1995 and helped lead the team that refunded Grateful Dead tickets through the fall of 1995 after Jerry's passing. Then he began working at GDTS TOO on the first Furthur Festival in spring 1996, before moving on.

Schofield remembers, "San Rafael in the early to mid-1980s was a very fun place to work—especially if you were employed by the Grateful Dead. It must have been what it was like in the Haight [in San Francisco] or maybe even real far back in Palo Alto, when the band just got started. San Rafael had a real neighborly feel, and the GDTS offices were in a funky building just a block or two from downtown. You saw the same people over and

over and were friendly with them on the street. Working for Grateful Dead Ticket Sales was like managing a hip clothing store, or operating a real popular lunch counter. Except, of course, *we* were working in rock and roll!"

Supervisor Tom Reed: "I joined up in March 1987 when the scene exploded around 'Touch of Grey.' I brought to GDTS a fierce and never-wavering loyalty to the music. I was only in the first ticketing office for a short while before we moved to 1110 Lincoln, the two-story house that is the stuff of ticketing legend. At 1110, Calico was in charge of the ticketing process that was downstairs, and I was in charge of getting the ticketed mail upstairs and made ready to send out. We used registered mail to ensure customers got their tickets safely.

"Of course, every one of those orders had to be handwritten into a postal book and then

Trolling the envelope archive at GDTS TOO. *Sandy Duveen photo*

brought to the post office for further processing. So I dealt with the USPS every day of the week and was granted virtually unprecedented access to San Rafael's main branch post office. I can say with certainty that my car and I handled at least one million pieces of mail while I was at GDTS—maybe considerably more!"

Joanne was the anchor of the upstairs crew handling customer service. With her inimitable Long Island voice, she had it all *down*. Where things bottlenecked was in the now quaint-sounding—really, analog—filing of the 3x5 index cards that kept track of every Dead Head's updated contact information and every order, whether filled or rejected for not following procedure or providing insufficient or fraudulent funds, or because the show was sold out.

"On a busy day," continued Tom, "we'd have to file at least one thousand cards, sometimes twice that. No one liked to file cards because it was a complete pain in the ass. So, some time every day while we were working shows and ticketing and registering and going full speed ahead, I would have to go downstairs and as gently as possible cause a cessation to the ticketing process so that *all* of us—sometimes excluding Steven and Frankie, who were involved in their own madnesses—would help with the painstaking task of filing all those cards alphabetically. There had to be this accuracy so that Joanne and I—we were the main people who, under aliases that became well-known to the fans, answered the customer-service phones—could give correct information to Dead Heads calling in to find out if their order had been filled or not.

"Not every day but often, Calico and I would butt heads; she didn't want to be taken off task. She and I were—are—very driven and stubborn individuals, but the filing did get done and Calico and I would lick our wounds and come back the next day for more. Both Calico and I were dedicated to finishing our work and finishing it close to perfect . . . and it was very nearly perfect work we did.

"Picking up the mail at the post office and bringing it back to GDTS—that was 99 percent

me. Beginning work on an upcoming tour, when the mail hit, it was generally 50 to 70 trays of mail, with about 300 to 325 envelopes in each tray. So, 20,000 letters or more arriving all at once was common for us. Much of it, maybe 60 percent, was decorated by the Dead Heads. And it all went in my car—which is why it's not at all far fetched to say that my car carried over a million letters total, not even factoring in the value of the money orders.

"Once those 50 to 70 trays hit the office, Calico, Forrest, and I—with our crews—sorted by postmark and venue and as in the case of, say, Madison Square Garden, we'd sort by which series of three shows the orders were for. Sorting mail at that volume, doing it for ten hours with requisite smoke breaks, left us mentally numb at the finish of a day. And, of course, every single ticket-request letter that came in ultimately would generate a letter going out.

"Think about it. One announcement from an unlisted phone bank would generate sometimes more than a million dollars of orders six or seven days afterwards. This would happen over and over again. I truly feel that if the band was still intact and touring like they did, with merchandise and tickets in full swing, the Grateful Dead likely would be generating a billion dollars per year now. You can imagine, this was heady stuff for us all, being responsible for tens of millions of dollars in repeated transactions.

"Let me also say this: GDTS was fun, it was grueling, it was rewarding, and the intense vortex our collective energy created was a kind of high that not too many folks ever get to experience at their day job."

Supervisor Mary Knudsen, a near Olympic-qualifying women's softball team first baseman, started work in April 1987 and later helped GDTS TOO get started in 1996. "My brother Ron was already working for GDTS around the time of 'Touch of Grey,'" she recalls. "He mentioned they probably would want help, as they were anticipating a truckload of ticket requests for the next tour. Frankie asked if I wanted to pitch in. I happily said yes.

Honoring ticket requests at GDTS TOO, early 2011.
Sandy Duveen photo

"Amazingly, I commuted all the way from Hayward, many miles across the Bay. My hours increased once my softball program and college classes were done, and it was a gleeful day when I began working full time. I would supervise the money collection procedures—you can imagine, depositing money is *the* key to any successful mail order operation. If a team member was having trouble balancing their collection of money orders, I'd be there to help. When I wasn't preparing the deposits for the bank, I'd also fill orders.

"The job was so much fun—everyone working in close proximity, collaborating in furious waves to get tens of thousands of tickets out the door, and millions of dollars to the bank. Yet, we'd listen to music and have great conversations as we opened the gazillion envelopes and made hundreds of piles. I don't think anything will ever compare to the joyful insanity of Grateful Dead ticketing!"

As the music rose from the ashes of the Grateful Dead after Jerry's passing, in the form of the Furthur Festival, Rat Dog, Phil Lesh & Friends, the Other Ones, Planet Drum, the TriChromes, The Dead, and Furthur with Phil Lesh and Bob Weir, loyal Dead Heads continued to send in for tickets as if nothing in their world, or in the ticketing procedures (which included their self-motivated decoration of envelopes), had ever changed.

Because of the value that it held to the fans, and because a strong income stream could continue on, the remaining members of the band gift-shared the ticket office to the most tenured employees rather than disband GDTS entirely when the announcement was made that they would no longer tour under the name Grateful Dead.

"We came to the conclusion," the press release read, "that the 'long strange trip' of the uniquely wonderful beast known as the Grateful Dead was over. Although individually and in various combinations we will undoubtedly continue to make music, whatever the future holds will be something different in name and structure. While we won't be playing under the name Grateful Dead, we're still going to be plenty busy."

The desire to continue keeping "plenty busy" meant that on April 1, 1996, GDTS TOO, Inc. became officially an employee owned S corporation. Two key principals emerged as owners: Frankie Accardi-Peri and Calico Van Der Mei, united in their continued devotion to serving the Dead Heads in the spirit of what they agreed was still a unique community.

Calico ("Ruby" as the Dead Heads would know her in the context of her longtime ticketing prowess) and Frankie worked together as partners for nine years, forming a deep friendship. Frankie said, "It was almost unspoken. We understood each others' professional style and we were both dedicated to maintaining a smooth bus ride, you know, as the song goes, the *bus to never-everland*."

Calico handled the ticketing procedure, customer service, and updating the mailing list. Frankie administered the office operations; contacted promoters and venues; secured the necessary allotment of tickets, sometimes bucking promoter interference; settled the shows; developed the GDTS web-page design; and—most critically—balanced the books.

Frankie Accardi-Peri, Tom Reed, Carol Latvala, Steven Marcus, and Joanne Wishnoff reunite in San Rafael, March 2011. *Author photo*

What with all her procedural duties, the love of music and love for the scene still reigned over all. "High among my most fun and most innovative projects has been the artistic design of our tickets, which you see with our beautiful commemorative New Year's Eve and special-event tickets," said Frankie. "Graphics that bring a smile to your face express what we do best."

As orders came in with each new tour, the percentage of beautifully decorated envelopes actually increased. The passion displayed in the Dead Heads' art inspired the first of many "Fabulous Envelope" contests. One primary motivation was that the winner for a particular tour's worth of artistry would receive two complimentary tickets to the show of their choice.

The result of the contests is that hundreds more eye-opening pieces were generated, some of which are depicted in this chapter.

"Even the USPS postal clerks left notes judging their favorites," said Frankie. "And I do have to thank the employees in all the branch post offices where we opened P.O. boxes—from San Rafael, to other cities in Marin, and ultimately to the current Stinson Beach post office—because they've been so helpful in dealing with the repeated onslaughts of mail. They've also been very candid about their appreciation for the envelope decorations, and

that's saying something—because some of the most beautiful also are the most difficult to decipher, address-wise. Overall, what has come about is a tapestry of what is uniquely *Grateful Dead*."

Calico retired in 2008 and Frankie has now gone it alone, rehiring some of the GDTS personnel and, now, their children. Three generations of Accardis and Accardi-Peris have worked in the ticket office. Frankie herself began working for GDTS in February 1984 and scarcely six months later was asked to co-manage with Steven.

The years flew by in quick succession, and in 2011, in part because GDTS TOO networks with box office managers all over the United States and Canada, Frankie was honored with the lifetime professional achievement award from INTIX, the premiere international ticket association.

And so it goes. The Grateful Dead's former band members' newest incarnation is Futhur. It performed three tours in 2010, playing over eighty shows in sixty different venues, including highly anticipated New Year's Eve performances. Fair access to good seats, with only modest service charges, remains the company's credo. Sustaining the work of the band members and their affiliated musicians and charities continues. GDTS TOO, Inc. is still the world's finest fan-motivated ticketing operation of its kind. Same as it ever was.

TOP: *Don Berger, GDTS TOO collection*

BOTTOM: *Kim Cuzzilla, GDTS TOO collection*

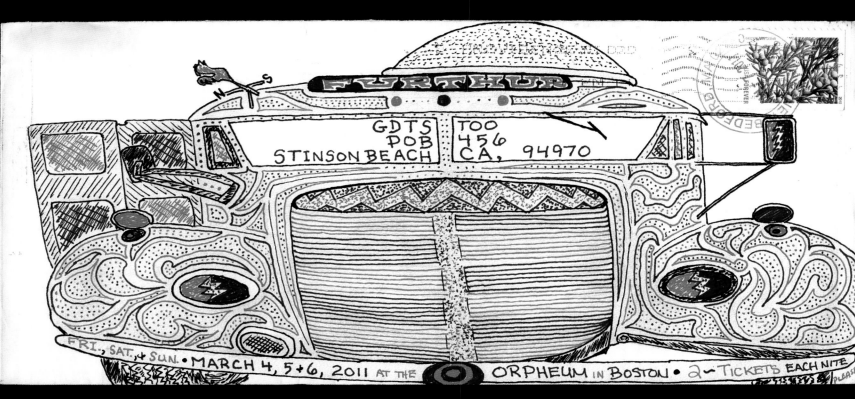

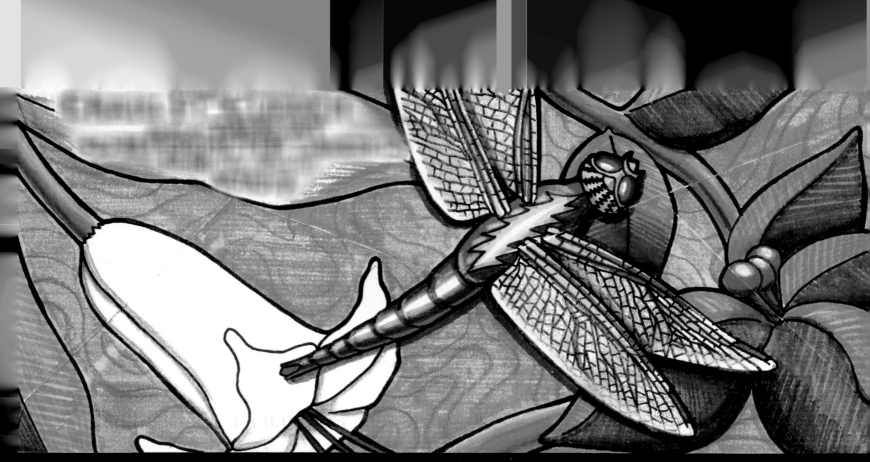

TOP: *Ted Frazier, GDTS TOO collection*

BOTTOM: *Gaby Cuellar, GDTS TOO collection*

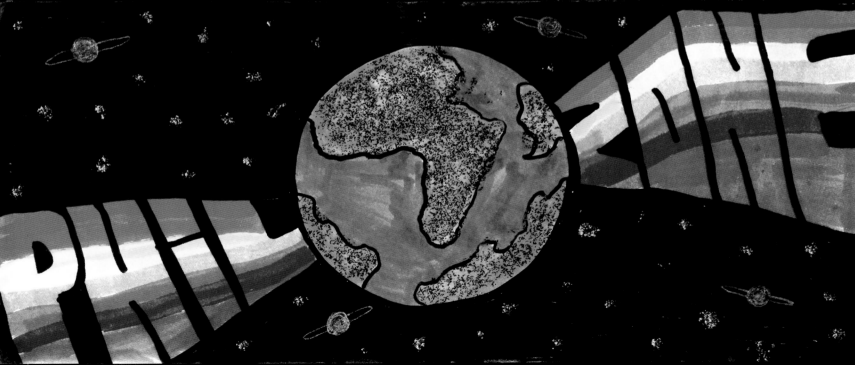

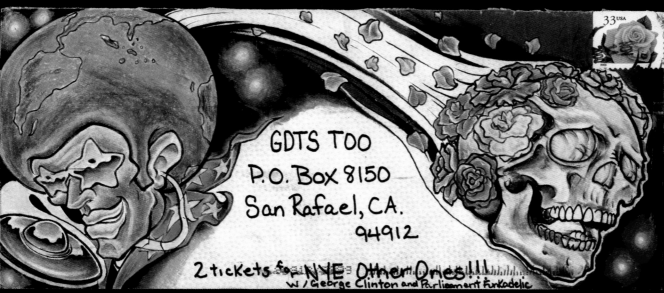

TOP: *Samonberry Mariposa, GDTS TOO collection*

BOTTOM: *Brian Virgin, GDTS TOO collection*

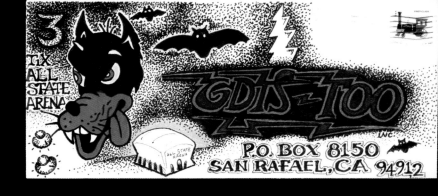

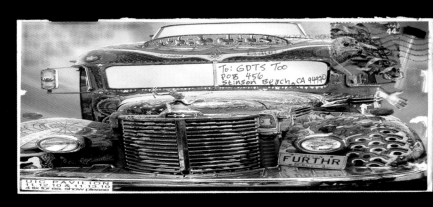

TOP: *Jim Kawski, GDTS TOO collection*   BOTTOM: *Lyerly Tuck, GDTS TOO collection*

TOP: *Jeff Weyer, GDTS TOO collection*   BOTTOM: *Erik Sagerstrom, GDTS TOO collection*

MIDDLE: *Regina Smith, GDTS TOO collection*

MIDDLE: *Glen Power, GDTS TOO collection*

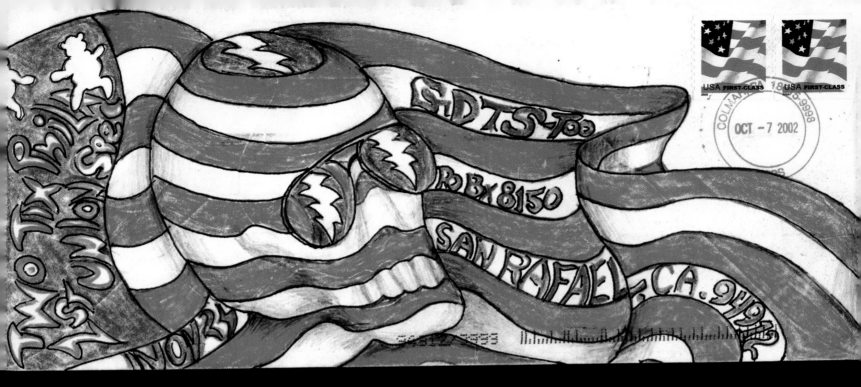

TOP LEFT: *Desiree Dodson, GDTS TOO collection*

BOTTOM LEFT: *Kevin Coley, GDTS TOO collection*

RIGHT: *Samonberry Mariposa, GDTS TOO collection*

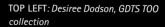

TOP LEFT: *Miki Saito, GDTS TOO collection*

BOTTOM LEFT: *L. Miller, Camden, GDTS TOO collection*

TOP RIGHT: *Julie Cathie, GDTS TOO collection*

BOTTOM RIGHT: *Amy Felbinger, GDTS TOO collection*

203

Epilogue

"A Dead-Letter Day" was the headline to the April 25, 2008, story in the *San Jose Mercury News* reporting that the Grateful Dead Archive would be donated by the band to the University of California, Santa Cruz.

The entire collection (not including the separate concert tape library) was received and housed at UCSC within the following year. Then, work began to catalog, preserve, and eventually make everything accessible in Special Collections at the renovated McHenry Library in the middle of the vast, forested campus high above the Pacific Ocean. The resource was tentatively called "Dead Central."

"All this stuff—what Eileen Law collected on our behalf or, better yet, what she didn't allow us to throw away—doesn't belong to us," said Bob Weir at the news conference announcing the band's gift. "It belongs to the culture that spawned us.

"It seemed like getting it into a campus archive, with access for the people in the larger Bay Area and American social community that gave rise to it, was the right thing to do. The Dead discovered a new land, a new place, and these folks at UCSC are the cartographers and are going to map it out."

Head of mapping, so to speak, is UCSC archivist Nicholas G. Meriwether, who moved from a similar position at the University of South Carolina to take on the task of cataloguing the collection and determining how it can be shared and showcased. Meriwether is a published author on several Grateful Dead topics, and his knowledge, care, and passion are undeniable. He is also determined to grow the collection further by appealing to all the Dead Heads in the world to consider deeding their collections to UCSC when ready.

The final boxes were packed in April 2009, and many truckloads were delivered. With the last big rig pawing at the gravel, anxious to leave one last time for Santa Cruz, the doors to the 2,000-square-foot warehouse in San Rafael were locked down for good.

That warehouse—a far cry from her original hole-in-the-wall at the band's headquarters, set up after the 1971 "Dead Freaks Unite" message was delivered to the world—had been Eileen's last official lair. Here in San Rafael, for thirty-five years, she responded to the band's direction that she collect all the press clippings, maintain the album, CD, and DVD holdings, and interact with the Dead Heads. Early on in her employment she personally took charge of saving "what needed to be saved." Although she was not responsible for putting aside the best of the decorated ticket-request envelopes, she (along with Dennis McNally, Alan Trist, Danny Rifkin, Willy Legate, Dick Latvala, and others) became one of the band's de facto historians and, in some respects, the band's historical conscience.

(The Dead's equally vast trove of their own concert recordings are stored in a Southern

California vault belonging to Rhino Entertainment, which administers the Dead's official releases.)

The trucks all having arrived, the UCSC Special Collections Department began taking stock of its 100,000 new items. The collection certainly contained what UCSC chancellor George Blumenthal called "valuable artifacts that document the band's ascendance into one of California's most durable and influential musical phenomena."

Examples of the artifacts include the 15,000 Dead Head–decorated ticket-request envelopes; the Dead's first recording contract and its extensive correspondence with its first record company (Warner Bros.); life-size skeletons of the band members used in the 1987 "Touch of Grey" video; and thousands more Dead Head–created photos, poems, artworks, and reminiscences.

Also included were the band's stash of vinyl recordings, CDs, DVDs, and videos; the original cassette tapes of Hotline messages announcing tour dates; and the show guest lists. Minutes of the band's official board meetings were deep in the boxes as well.

"What you'll see at the archive is our conversation with the people who loved us, and vice versa," said Mickey Hart, also representing the band at the announcement ceremony, held at the original San Francisco Fillmore Auditorium where the Dead had played forty-six times between 1965 and 1969. "The love affair and the dance that

Dawn Laurant, curator of the Marin History Museum, at the Grateful Dead Archive warehouse in Novato, before the move to UCSC. Eileen Law, head of the archives, is behind her. *Author photo*

the fans and us had are all contained in here. And it takes a place like UCSC, which has soul, in our opinion, to make something really creative and useful come of it.

"If you want to know how the Dead were built, this is where you'll go. You'll see how we put the business together. You'll find out the hopes and dreams of a bunch of weirdos that were blindly going someplace together. It's our whole story."

"The Dead were the quintessential American band," said Fred Lieberman, a UCSC music professor, who first proposed the university-housed archive idea to Hart (and co-wrote several books with him). "This is an important step toward having a dedicated library that is a destination for scholars interested in studying an important aspect of America's vernacular music." Hart's conversations with Lieberman would begin to flesh out Eileen's dream solution.

"I was the person who never shredded," Eileen said. "It started off in my little closet at the Dead's headquarters at 5th and Lincoln and it kept growing . . . and growing . . . and never stopped growing. Pretty soon—like within the first six months—I found myself being the keeper of everything the band and I thought important—all the press clippings, the concert posters and handbills, all the band's vinyl. But I also realized it was pretty much up to me to stash away the letters. Year after year, it became harder to find a place big enough to put it all away. Everything I could collect, I did; but where was the space and the funding to care for it long term? But I also had faith that something good would someday happen to it, that a museum or a library would take notice."

The UCSC McHenry Library will have a dedicated, interactive reading room, the basis for Dead Central, with music accessible on headphones and featuring rotating exhibitions. All the Grateful Dead holdings will be digitally captured and much will appear in due course on a new university-run website, the Virtual Terrapin Station. A large grant from the Institute of Museum and Library Services is making the scanning possible.

"I think it's a perfect fit for UC Santa Cruz, Santa Cruz itself, and by extension Northern California from which the band emerged," said Christine Bunting, head of special collections for the library. "The collection is all about the ethos of the band, the whole idea of community sharing, and that is really well matched with our campus. We have an excellent music program, and in a cross-disciplinary way there is great interest in the study of American vernacular music and popular culture.

"We also have this whole side that's concerned with social justice and tolerance and community spirit. And I think that fits so perfectly with what the band has done and what the Dead Heads have sustained over the years.

"What we're building will provide extraordinary opportunities for researchers and

the public to examine the music of one of the most influential bands in history, as well as explore the cultural phenomenon of the Dead Heads—the most dedicated and celebrated fans in music.

"Already we've contributed hugely to two projects: the well-attended and long-running exhibition coordinated by the New York Historical Society, and of course this book!"

How does Eileen really feel about letting go of the archive she tended all those years? "It's a bit ironic, like actually sending your kids off to college: 'Oh, they're leaving home!' I think of it this way, the collection is just getting ready for its next stage of development. Now it can continue to grow!"

Nick Meriwether is optimistic that, among all of the great rock bands with decades of history behind them, the Dead have found the ideal solution—a university library—to bear witness to a culture they were instrumental in creating. "Now, imagine if everyone involved, and I'm speaking of the Dead Heads here, were to join with us and share their memories and personal collections," he says. "We could have Terrapin Station for the ages! I think it's all about taking real seriously, taking to heart, the words of that noble American folksong 'This train. We are bound for glory, this train.'"

Acknowledgments

Thank You for a Real Good Time

Huge thanks all around. First, to the Grateful Dead band members who once again let me in to make a historic book. And here's to the souls of the departed: Jerry, Pig, Keith, Brent, Vince, BG, Don Pearson, Ram Rod, Hal Kant, Dick Latvala, Rex, and now Bear.

There's not sufficient space to thank everyone at Grateful Dead Productions and Ice Nine by title, but I was given tremendous support by, particularly, Eileen Law, David Lemieux, and Alan Trist.

People past and present at GDTS and GDTS TOO were greatly involved in the creation of *Dead Letters* and insisted on many an occasion, "this book needs to come out!" So, hugs and thanks to Frankie Accardi-Peri, Steven Marcus, Joanne Wishnoff, Carol Latvala, Forrest Schofield, Mary Knudsen, Tom Reed, and Michael Peri.

Mark Pinkus and Kelly Spinks at Rhino Entertainment cleared the way, as did Tim Jorstad, Eric Doney, and Peter McQuaid. I thank Bill Walton for the foreword, and Tom Stack, John Hareas, and Barry Axelrod for their assistance.

I also want to remember the contributions made over time by GDP's Danny Rifkin, Jon McIntire, Mary Ann Mayer, Nadine Kaplan, Rock Scully, Cameron Sears, Diane Geoppo, Nancy Mallonee, Rosie McGee, Steve Brown, Bill Candelario, Steve Parish, Sparky Raizene, and Patricia Harris. Also, the original fan club's Sue Swanson, Connie Bonner, and Bob Matthews.

I tip my hat to UCSC's Christine Bunting and Nick Meriwether in Special Collections and the Grateful Dead Archive, who will take all of this much Furthur. A further huzzah to Scott Campbell, who handled the scanning of the artifacts at UCSC.

I also want to thank my colleagues at BGP, my friends at Monarch, and my extended family at Live Nation Merchandise—especially Dell Furano, my mentor over some thirty years, who once told me, "Paul, you got to *teach 'em* how to rock and roll." Thanks also to LNM's (and Winterland's and Signatures') Phil Cussen, Michael Krassner, Rick Fish, Carl Walter, and Frank Vacanti.

Dead Letters came into the right hands at the right time, and I thank everyone at Voyageur Press, particularly editor Dennis Pernu, who handled Grateful Dead madness as well as anyone ever has. Thanks also to Voyageur Press publisher Michael Dregni, design manager LeAnn

Kuhlmann, designers Mighty Media, and publicist John Wurm.

Fellow historians kept me sane, including Blair Jackson, Regan McMahon, Dennis McNally, Steve Silberman, David Dodd, David Gans, and John W. Scott, Mike Dolgushkin, and Stu Nixon at Dead Base.

The contributions of photographers Jim Marshall, Jay Blakesberg, Sandy Duveen, Lisa Law (and Pilar Law), and Trevalyan Markle deserve a shout out, as do Norman Ruth at Terrapin Trailways and Deluxe Design, Wavy Gravy and Zappo at the Hog Farm, Jeff Wood at Drowning Creek, Bert Holman and the Allman Brothers Band, Paul Roidoulas at Liquid Blue, Marcus White at the Stinson Beach post office, and poster collector Paul Getchell.

I also want to underscore the artistry of Barry Haden, Dan Nettell, Barbara Carr, and Laura Dowling and honor the memory of Damian Strahl.

Many others provided guidance, access, or just plain friendship in the midst of all the weirdness, including Joan Baylie and Jim Mullins, Marlene Getchell, Susana Millman, Dennis King, Joel Selvin, Dawn Laurant, Cassidy Law-Sears, and Mary Eisenhart.

A big thumbs up to Kevin Wright at Cantoo Imaging in Point Richmond, to Canon for the PowerShot G6 camera, and to the inventor of sheet protectors—a humble product that saved my life on many a dark and stormy night.

I'd like to thank my brother Jonas Grushkin, whose photography studio is now in Durango, Colorado, and our friend Cynthia Bassett for partnering in *The Official Book of the Dead Heads*, as well as my sister Dena (once a Dead Head in Madison, Wisconsin, now a pioneering teacher on two continents) and her husband Paul Florczyk for the sustenance. Let me also give a long minute of loving remembrance to our parents Philip and Jean Grushkin who taught us that "books are friends."

My grown kids, Jessica and Jordan Grushkin, continue to be amused by Dad's tilting at the Grateful Dead windmill (they've listened to enough Dead in the car to know what *that's* all about). But it was the love of my life, Jane Eskilson, who once again said, "Do it!" Thank you, Jane, for all the years combined.

The book is dedicated to Calico Van Der Mei, whose constancy of belief in turning to the light underscores everything this book is, and to Eileen Law, whose work to save what needed to be saved did the Dead a solid and made this book actually possible. Eileen, you are my best buddy in all of Grateful Dead.

Voyageur Press and I made a valiant attempt to contact every Dead Head who has an envelope or envelopes represented within this book. However the vintage nature of the artworks made complete success in these attempts impossible. We received back many of our letters marked "return to sender," indicating quite a number of you have moved on over the past forty years. If your envelope or envelopes are included and you didn't hear from us, we'd love to hear from you.

Dead Letters is the result of a forty-six-year love fest—the appreciation the Dead Heads have had over all this time for a band beyond description. To all of you I say, *Reach out your hand*.

But truly, in closing, there are no better words than those of Pigpen's:

AND LEAVE IT ON!

Paul Grushkin
Pinole, California

About the Author

Sandy Duveen photo

Paul Grushkin is one of America's top rock music historians. His books have sold over one million copies worldwide.

For the past thirty years, Grushkin has been at the forefront of rock merchandising. As VP/sales and marketing and senior marketing consultant for Live Nation Merchandise (and previously Signatures Network, Sony Signatures, and Winterland Productions), he led the retail campaigns for nearly every top rock, pop, and country act, including the Beatles, John Lennon, Bruce Springsteen, Garth Brooks, Ozzy Osbourne, the Doors, Led Zeppelin, New Kids on the Block, Backstreet Boys, N'Sync, Reba McEntire, Alan Jackson, and more than 200 others.

Grushkin's previous books include: *Grateful Dead: The Official Book of the Dead Heads*, with Jonas Grushkin and Cynthia Bassett (1983); *The Art of Rock: Posters from Presley to Punk* (1987); *Treasures of the Hard Rock Café*, with Joel Selvin (2001); *Art of Modern Rock: The Poster Explosion*, with Dennis King (2004); *Rockin' Down the Highway: The Cars and People That Made Rock Roll* (2006); and *Art of Classic Rock: The Rob Roth Collection* (2009).

Grushkin is a graduate of Stanford University and was archivist for Bill Graham Presents. He is represented on the lecture tour circuit by Wolfman Productions. An East Coast native, he resides in the San Francisco Bay Area.

It Still Hasn't Gotten

Weird Enough For Me